W9-APD-563

DISCARD

DATE			

® THE BAKER & TAYLOR CO.

REPRIEVE

_____

A MEMOIR

Also by Agnes de Mille

AMERICA DANCES

WHERE THE WINGS GROW

SPEAK TO ME, DANCE WITH ME

RUSSIAN JOURNALS

DANCE IN AMERICA

THE BOOK OF THE DANCE

LIZZIE BORDEN: A DANCE OF DEATH

TO A YOUNG DANCER

AND PROMENADE HOME

DANCE TO THE PIPER

AGNES DE MILLE

Reprieve

A MEMOIR

Foreword and Notes
by Fred Plum, M.D.

Neurologist-in-Chief
The New York Hospital
Cornell Medical Center

DOUBLEDAY & COMPANY, INC., GARDEN CITY, NEW YORK
1981

Library of Congress Cataloging in Publication Data
ISBN: 0-385-15721-5
Library of Congress Catalog Card Number 81-43059
Copyright © 1981 by Agnes de Mille
All Rights Reserved
Printed in the United States of America
First Edition

To
The Staff of The New York Hospital
and in particular
the nurses
Hubertine Maas
and
Collette Quigley

FOREWORD

BY Fred Plum, M.D.

THIS BOOK delineates a profile in quiet bravery. Agnes de Mille suffered a serious stroke in 1975 while awaiting the opening curtain of her long-awaited, new show. For several weeks thereafter she wavered at the edge of death or overwhelming neurological catastrophe, but she indomitably kept her impertinent curiosity through even the worst hours. The acute illness left her with a severe degree of paralysis and sensory loss on her right side. Fortunately for her and the world, her mind and speech remained unscathed. As she worked and swore her way back from her disability, tolerating a degree of crippling that would have incapacitated a lesser personality, she simultaneously shifted to left-hand writing so as to complete the book she had already started when the brain hemorrhage struck. In the five years since her stroke, plagued by subsequent heart attack, severe residual weakness, and a neurological defect that sometimes prevents her even from knowing where her right arm or leg is located, this hearty septuagenarian has given some of her finest performances. Blocked by the stroke from giving a performance by Heritage Dance Theater, Agnes de Mille pulled herself and the concert together and staged a performance that, through television, has now reached millions in every corner of the United States. Forced to accept minuscule royalties and a barely mentioned artistic attribution in the first performance of *Oklahoma!* in 1943, she has seen herself acclaimed as one of the co-creators of that pioneering musical in its Broadway renaissance in 1979. During these past three years, via television, she has taught many their first lessons about the dance and all of us things we never knew before. Above all, she has taught all of us, patients, families and doctors alike, that while a stroke can mean a terrible detour in life, it need not mean the end. In this book Agnes de Mille tells the story of her illness.

A bit now about why I, the doctor, also speak in these pages. When Miss de Mille asked me to supply some technical details, I was privileged to join in, although I thought the medical efforts almost trivial when placed alongside her chronicle of resourcefulness and determination. Some may ask what leads a physician to abandon his traditional and natural reticence to broach a patient's dignity and discuss her illness as I do here. The answer is straightforward. Miss de Mille's medical recovery and subsequent return to new and brilliant professional accomplishments reflects no passively received benefits of a modern "medical miracle." Rather, they are the result of her own arduous efforts and refusal to be held down by mere physical handicaps. Despite a brain hemorrhage, followed by several small strokes, a pulmonary embolus, a subsequent heart attack, and residual neurological limitations which leave half of her body partly paralyzed and insensate, she has graduated from being a convalescent to living an innovative, independent, witty, humane life. For her, illness resides in the past rather than occupying the present. That example is worth our examination, for those who can learn from and follow it will enrich their own lives as Agnes de Mille has enriched hers and, by the radiance of her spirit, mine.

CONTENTS

INSULT

13

INJURY

153

CHALLENGE

269

PART ONE

Insult

Hail to thee, blithe spirit!
Bored thou never wert . . .
—WALTER PRUDE
AFTER SHELLEY

I

At 5:50 p.m. on May 15, 1975, I stood in the auditorium of the Hunter College Playhouse in New York City giving last-minute instructions to my dance company before a lecture-dance concert. The concert was sold out and the audience numbered quite the most elite and distinguished people in New York.

Suddenly I discovered that half of my body was dead.

For the benefit of readers not familiar with recent American dance careers, let me recapitulate a few facts: I was well known as a concert and ballet dancer in the first decade of my career, and particularly known as an actress and comedienne. I also was blessed with extremely fleet and neat feet and therefore remarkably strong point work. In the middle period of my career I choreographed ballets for Broadway musicals and became for a time the most successful and best known choreographer in

America. Later I specialized in ballets and latterly I had
spent all of my energies in trying to establish the Agnes
de Mille Heritage Dance Theater, which was devoted ex-
clusively to dances of American traditional and historical
interest. In this endeavor I met with many obstacles. The
vogue in the seventies was for Russian and European
ballet dancing or, alternately, the very far-out modern
work. Traditional American forms were definitively felt to
be outmoded.

But now matters seemed to be improving. Certain crit-
ics had sprung to my defense and to the defense of the
Heritage Dance Theater. The government and a few
large foundations had signified interest. Monies were
promised. IBM had agreed to give us over one hundred
thousand dollars for a TV program of one hour's length.
The Shubert Foundation, very wealthy and reasonably
powerful, declared itself concerned. And the Rockefeller
Foundation, which had aided us in the past, continued to
keep a fatherly eye on our endeavors. All the important
people involved—the board of IBM, the board of the Shubert Foundation, prominent members of the Rockefeller
Foundation, representatives of the United States Government and the New York State Council on the Arts and important and powerful individuals—had taken tickets to
the May 15 program and promised to come, had even
asked for tickets for their friends and relatives (free, of
course); they were, in fact, at that moment having dinner
and preparing to leave their homes. It was to be the deci-
sive night in our adventures and I dearly wanted it to be

a success because everything we had worked for for years, and all the money that had been lent us, and my entire time had been bent toward this one project. The twenty-six dancers were ready; the guest stars were ready. I had proven a forceful speaker. I hoped I was ready.

To say it was a lecture is misleading: I talked alright and quite a lot. But the points were illustrated by twenty-six able dancers, some of them stars: Honi Coles, for instance; Hortense Koulouris, a pupil of Isadora Duncan; Gemze de Lappe of Broadway fame; Victor Wellesly, Scotch and Irish world champion at the Highland Games; Linda Di Bona, ballerina of the Harkness Company; Buzz Miller and Ethel Martin, leads with Jack Cole; and nineteen members of my Heritage Theater. At the Steinway was a concert pianist, David Baker.

Still, it was dangerous to hazard so much of our fortunes on the well-being of one individual, and in the past, when I had taken on any comparable responsibility, the manager, Sol Hurok, had carried large insurance on me. But now I could afford no such luxury and we took the risk, although I was much older and I was tired. Yet we took the chance. There was no choice.

May 15 is the twenty-first birthday of one of the most beautiful members of the Heritage cast, Delight Walters. The dancer John Giffen accompanied me to the theater, carrying the very large birthday cake on his knees and helping with the shopping bags full of paper cups, plastic spoons, napkins, etc. And the stage manager was given money to buy wine. John Giffen was dispatched for ice. Immediately after the performance and the surprise birthday party, I was to go to the Charles Holleriths', who were giving me a gala supper to celebrate what we hoped would be the end of the Heritage Theater's financial and business troubles. The hosts had gone to the most enormous pains and expense for this. It was to be an evening of celebration.

I was at the theater three hours before curtain, nervous, naturally. I always am. This time I seemed not to be quite as excited as usual, slightly dulled but keyed up in a strange way, as though I had lost interest and was pushing myself to keep my attention on the business at hand. But I knew the dullness would pass off once I walked on the stage. I was in my street dress and shoes. My lecture dress, my beautiful red dress designed by Stanley Simmons, was being pressed in the wardrobe room. The black opal my husband had brought me from Australia was in my purse, together with my false eyelashes. After last-minute instructions, I planned to put on makeup and be quiet. I had better be; the show lasted two hours and I would speak with only the barest notes, mainly music cues. I spaced the dancers around the stage, briefed them, and then began to arrange the bows, but I lost interest as I lost interest in the blasphemous and quarrelsome wrangling of two guest artists. I offered to sign the contract of the new member of the cast, summoned on emergency. I was handed the AGMA contract and I took out my pen.

And I couldn't write!

I said to the cast and to the dancers, "I can't write." And I looked around in surprise. "My hand won't work."

There should have been a thunderclap or a pang, but there was nothing. "If I should die before I wake . . . ," "If I should die before my next breath . . . or before I sign my name." There was no pain, no sensation of any kind, no warning. Indeed, I'm not even sure what happened. Simply I discovered I could not write and threw down the pen. Maybe it had happened sooner. But once I knew, once I was aware, I was on a toboggan and events raced. I felt no different after than before. In the recent play *Wings,* by Arthur Kopit, Constance Cummings, who played the heroine, suffers a stroke as she sits center stage in a spotlight. Bells go off, sirens scream. There is a great jangling and flashing of lights, enormous din and confusion, and I suppose this is the author's way of indicating the huge reversal of her entire natural processes and the revolution in her body. But actually there are no clues, there is no warning, and that is its sinister dreadfulness, the unsuspected catastrophe which catches one unwarily in the middle of life and drops one unsuspectingly into the pit. I said, quietly, "My hand won't work. I can't write." The people around me said, "Sit down and be quiet." There were no bells.

David Baker, the pianist, remembers this moment. "Nothing had seemed to go well, and she had been raging with all too much energy for something to work—the lights, the tapes, the dancing. And nothing much *was* working. Finally she dismissed the company with just enough time to grab a sandwich and be ready for the performance. I came down off the stage to sit with her in about the third row on the aisle. I suppose she was trying to pull herself together and find some new source of energy for the performance. In any event, she was not to be comforted by me or anyone else. After a few moments she turned to me and said, 'I have no feeling in my right leg.' But quietly. I remember thinking that anyone would be in a state after that rehearsal, so I was not alarmed and told her to sit quietly for a minute, and which she did. It would pass, I said."

I'm told that I was flushed and that I looked hectic. And then I said to my good friend Mary Green, "I can't feel on the right side. Maybe we'd better have a doctor." And I thought, "This is very interesting. This is curious." I sat and waited. And then I said, "I'm cold." And David Guthrie, who was in charge of costumes, took off his coat and put it around me. It was a warm May evening and nobody was cold, but I sat shivering and I said, "Mary, I can't feel."

She said, "You're moving your foot and hand."

"But I can't feel. Am I talking funny? I seem to be talking funny."

David remembers: "I sat with her holding her hand and trying to be of some use, and what I remember most is that she seemed to know what was happening and she had no panic, that she would deal with this as she had dealt with other crises in her life."

Well, maybe. I gave my doctor's name and hospital. I was not aware of the dancers. They sat apart somewhat, just out of vision, silent, cowed, apprehensive. They sat without speaking, I think, watching to see what would happen.

John Giffen returned with the ice. "Here it is!" he said happily. "I've got it. Now we have everything." And he stopped, silenced. The theater seemed to have come to a halt.

The only person who moved about—and I watched her with unseeing eyes—was tiny Judy Epstein, who kept practicing chaîné pirouettes round and round the stage and back and forth, learning the floor surface, learning the dimensions. She had not been told there would be no performance. She was getting ready to give the performance we had planned to give. She never tired, she never stopped, round and round.

The secretary of Hunter College had very shrewdly sent for an ambulance.

Suddenly there was another voice beside me. "Agnes, this is George Gorham, your doctor, Gorham. I'll take care of you. Tell me what's the matter."

Dr. Gorham had received the summons on his beep box just as he was walking out the door of the hospital for his weekend vacation; and as The New York Hospital is only four blocks east of Hunter College, he reached me within minutes. I told him how I felt, which was lousy, and added, "Please do something fast because I've got to be on the stage in one hour delivering a very difficult lecture

and I've never been late for anything in the theater in my
life. Also, I must be bright."

He looked at me very gently and quietly and said, "You
won't be on the stage and you will be late."

And I said, "No concert?"

And he said, "No concert." Oddly enough, my feeling
at that moment was only one of great relief.

"Lie back," he said.

They carried me out and put me in a chair and carried
the chair out of the theater. The last I remember of that
place was the face of David Evans entering with his
makeup kit. He gaped with horror at the cortege passing,
me in a chair carried by attendants to the waiting ambulance with its revolving lights and its siren wailing. Mary
was frightened by the way my head lolled back and
flopped around. (She kept notes which have been of enormous help in writing this.)

Right at that moment the life pattern of about twenty-
seven young people altered—for several permanently. My
company was composed of difficult-to-hire youngsters, in
a sense misfits, although highly trained and good-looking.
They were not great ballet dancers; they were not orthodox, trained modern dancers; they could not fit in and
were therefore not suitable in the established groups. But
they were brilliant stage craftsmen with sound techniques,
and some of them had fine gifts as actors and comedians.
Together we were going to make the Heritage Theater a
known and beautiful thing. Now they sat huddled in the
auditorium like a clot of frightened children not knowing

what to do, discussing hysterically the possibilities of continuing the performance without me, which they very soon decided was an impossibility. The company manager, Don Tirabassi, and the producer and manager, Jean Dalrymple and Lillian Libman, rushed to the box office to start giving money back. There was shortly pandemonium. The dancers remained in a dismayed group, not daring to leave, not daring to ask. Nobody told them anything. Indeed, nobody knew anything.

The audience found out mostly by accident. John Houseman learned early and rushed to forestall the arrival of Richard Rodgers and his wife, Dorothy. Vera Maxwell learned as she stepped into the lobby and went home to await the phone call from my sister, Margaret, in Maryland, which she knew would surely come, the phone call begging for asylum in New York. My husband arrived at the theater to wish me good luck, to wish the cast good luck, to inquire if he could help, and walked into chaos, wild rumors flying and panic backstage. He was dispatched to the emergency ward of The New York Hospital.

The Holleriths, who were to be the hosts of the party, went home and dolefully received what stragglers still cared to celebrate—well, what stragglers felt like a very good supper in a very beautiful house with bounteous liquor. I am told the mood was subdued.

The first news bulletins were coming off the air.

The New York *Times* had its obit ready and Walter Terry, the dance critic, was notified to get his summation piece for the *Saturday Review*.

I had been taken away in the ambulance with my doctor, George Gorham, and with Mary Green and the pianist David Baker, all of whom, with great determination, had very quietly just entered the ambulance and come along.

In the ambulance, with bell clanging and siren screaming, the attendants had taken over and instantly started the rapid-fire interrogation which they always administer on these occasions, the routine questions to check on the exact state of memory and wits. What was my name? Where was I born? When was I born? Who was the President of the United States? What was this (holding up a wristwatch)? What day of the week was it? My answers grew consistently more vague. But to one, which was about my age, there was absolute silence. I was not going to tell these young men my age, any more than I'd tell reporters my age! They finally became exasperated and said, "Well, are you fifty-five?"

"Yes."

"Are you sixty-five?"

"Yes."

"Are you seventy-five?"

"Yes."

"Are you eighty-five?" I smiled at them. They shrugged and started over. This much I took in quite clearly; it was a source of great satisfaction to me.

Blood pressure was being taken. Dr. Gorham asked, "What is it?" The attendant told him and I remarked, "That's *very* high!"

Suddenly I emitted a sharp cry and everybody's face was brought into close focus.

"What!?"

"All that liquor! It goes to waste. The party!"

David Baker made the only comment he made on the whole trip. He spoke very soothingly and very quietly. "Agnes, did you ever know liquor to go to waste?"

"No," I said contentedly. "No, it will not go to waste."

"That's right," he said.

The wine was drunk, as David had said it would be, mainly by the stagehands, the cake may have been eaten, or maybe it was taken home by Delight. The dancers dispersed—having wept and having whispered in subdued voices—to their frightened solitude. Their ways were going to be very different after this night. The chief electrician, a boy from North Carolina, gathered up all light charts and all the paraphernalia and props and took them to my apartment, where he left them safely bundled up. The costumes—all of them—were collected by the new costume mistress, who carried them off to her own place of work, a theater, and guarded them in perfect security for one year. Judy Epstein didn't weep, nor gossip, nor wonder. She quietly went home and wrote down in detail all the new dances, the dances I had never seen on the stage, and so preserved them from oblivion.

"What day of the week was it? What is this (holding up a fountain pen)? Name the presidents going backward from Ford to Coolidge."

"Oh, please don't." I turned my head wearily away.

It was somewhere about this point that Mary noticed my right arm drop and hang nerveless at my side. It has never moved again with feeling or intelligence.

When we arrived at Gorham's hospital (The New York Hospital has no ambulance service of its own, and in this case they used the Lenox Hill's), which surprised the ambulance attendants because they expected to go to quite another hospital, Gorham said, "I'll take over." They objected strenuously and said they had charge and the young doctor in the ambulance said I was his patient. Gorham didn't even bother to answer.

Mary remembers it differently. I think my mind had started to close down. She said, "Those men had two aims: The driver intended to get Agnes to the hospital as fast as he could do so with safety; the ambulance attendant intended to keep her alive until he could turn her over to the hospital. They both did their jobs selflessly and superbly. The attendant worked constantly with and over her, taking blood pressure, pulse, asking questions. I don't think he had the time or free hands to take notes. The transfer from the ambulance to the hospital attendants, who were waiting, was quick, quiet—as smooth as silk. Someone even thought to tell me to duck and not bump my head getting out of the ambulance. Agnes and I were holding hands as she was wheeled in on a stretcher. It was pushed swiftly through open doors, me half-running alongside, hanging onto her right hand. We got to the inner doors and someone gently unclutched our hands and they wheeled Agnes through and the doors closed and I was standing there all alone and I began to shake. And I shook and shook all over like an old jalopy. David came and put his arm around me and held me quiet."

I recall very clearly being laid in bed. I said to Mary, who was standing beside me, "I am going to be bored, so terribly bored." And I never said an untruer word in my life. I was a lot of things in the near future, but I was not at any time bored.

This is the last time, Mary says, that she heard me speak clearly and with my unique timbre. Mary must take over. I drifted away.

"Doctors and nurses started coming and David and I shuffled around in the hall feeling useless. David said, 'I think I should tell them that she is Agnes de Mille, don't you?' I agreed. David pulled a sleeve and spoke to them. One of the doctors nodded offhandedly and they went right on talking. They had more important things to think about right then."

They couldn't have cared less about who I was or what I was. They cared as little as master plumbers confronted with a nasty stoppage in the pipes who are suddenly asked, in the middle of the dirt and mess, to note the color of the owner's eyes.

They took me away and brought me back. And they took me away again.

It was still only 7:15 P.M.

Matters seemed to be worsening. It was my luck that Gorham had summoned the doctors that he did to receive and help me because I was in trouble. Fortunately, right from the start I had good diagnoses and superb care. My luck extended to this: There was a brain scanner in the hospital, one of three such machines in the world and the only one at that time in New York, and it was at the moment available, and so I was taken in and laid in it. I had no memory of this because by this time my mind functioned only intermittently. What was the matter with me became apparent to them very quickly.

The room in which the enormous X-ray camera operated was exactly opposite the room in which they had placed me. When I was taken to be photographed, Walter arrived and was invited by the doctors to sit with them and watch the picture of my brain build up square by square, exposure by exposure. The blot showed, large as a walnut and definite and augmenting all the time. Gorham sat beside him.

There were murmurs.

"This is speech, possibly sight." There was more. "That is all speech and mobility." The blood increased. The blot grew. More, more. The doctor stopped the machine. Gorham took Walter into the hall.

"You must brace yourself. This is fatal."

Walter was not prepared for this. I was not prepared. It was drumhead trial and immediate execution.

Walter seemed somehow standing near me, his face luminous with compassion. And they laid me down and I took my left hand and patted my right leg, which felt nothing, and then I said, "Better, better." And Walter's eyes filled and he turned his head away.

He had just been told by two doctors, the head doctors, that they had found blood in my spinal canal fluid, and that I was not going to live the night.

I said, patting my right side, "Better, better." And I nodded my head a little and tried to smile.

Twenty-four hours earlier he had sat in a Chinese restaurant drinking to the theatrical success of his now huddled wreck. He left behind at home that morning a perfectly sane woman, excited by the impending event and by the imminence of nervous stress and responsibility and the chance of success, but happy and making lists of birthday parties and presents and tickets and items to take to the theater and problems to talk over with the musician, script spread in front of her, studying, memorizing. And he found now a depersonalized lump that could hardly babble her name and had begun to drool, an aged, crouched husk of a creature, seemingly moribund except when asked its name and then brightening up as pert as a parrot and snapping back the correct response.

Walter sat holding my hand.

A few people from the audience had gathered in the waiting room on the fourteenth floor to see what would happen: Margaret ("Good to the last drop") Hamilton, who played the Wicked Witch of the North in *The Wizard of Oz;* Morton Gould, the composer; David Baker and his friends; James Mitchell, the actor. Margaret still clutched the flowers she had brought to the theater; the

poor things were sent in to me, but it was not until the
next day that anyone thought to put them into water. The
good friends remained quietly. The acquaintances chattered loudly; some laughed vociferously.

Mary remembers, "I kept watching for Walter, jumping up when anybody came in or passed by. I saw Dr.
Gorham a couple of times and had to hold myself to keep
from asking questions. At last Walter came. He was gray.
He said, 'We don't know anything certain yet.' Walter
went and we, our little group, made small talk.

'Mary, what a pretty dress.'

'Thank you. I used to wear it in college.'

'My God, just shows that simple lines last.'

'Yeah, and it's made on the bias so it still fits.'

'Lordy, it's hot.'

'D'you know it's going to rain?'

'Did anyone hear a forecast?'

'No.'

'Yes.'

'Those guys are never right.'

'It's an imprecise science.'"

I'm told Walter turned his chair with his back to them
and sat looking out the window into the spring evening.
His silence, Morton Gould said, was heartbreaking. The
one visitor allowed into my room and brought to me by
my husband was Charles Dubin, the director, here from
Hollywood to prepare our Heritage program for television, which IBM was going to sponsor. "Don't be shocked
when you go in," warned Mary. "Her speech is going."

He took my hand, the left one, the feeling one, and kissed me and said, "Anytime you're ready, whenever you're ready, just tell me and I'll come from wherever I am." I made some gargling noises, but he smiled at me and he kissed me again. He was weeping when he went into the hall. And then he left and the night continued. Walter held my hand; the lights dimmed.

He had advised the faithful to go home. It would be long, he said, and there would be nothing they could do. And so they left and Walter told Mary Green to please put in two phone calls, one to our son, Jonathan, in Cambridge, and one to my sister, Margaret, in Easton, Maryland. Later Mary got through to Jonathan, but not until two in the morning, and he said he would start driving immediately. She implored him to come any way he wished but not to drive himself. My sister had just returned to Easton from New York, where she had been undergoing painful and frightening chemotherapy for cancer. She was exhausted, sick, and very weak, but she got a friend to drive her to the Baltimore airport.

It was Walter who remembered to get me a private nurse, which no one else had thought to do. It was 8:15 P.M.; the curtain would have just about been going up. No one had thought to send word to the dancers.

Having made her call, Mary returned.

On the empty fourteenth floor of The New York Hospital the desk nurse tried to stop her. "Wait a minute. You're not supposed to be here." "Well, I *am* here," she said, and she didn't turn her head as she hastened on and found Walter in the solarium. Mary had reported back after a fruitless visit to a completely wrong hospital, so great was her distress. "Walter was in a sort of reclining chair with his back to the door. We just sat quietly and every ten minutes or so a pretty little Filipino nurse came out and told Walter what Agnes' blood pressure was. It began to get light and Walter said that I must go home; and he went with me to the lobby and the man at the desk called a cab. While we waited, day broke and the lobby and the streets were empty. And I thought, as I pulled away, seeing him standing there all alone at the entrance, that he was one of the loneliest sights I've ever seen."

Walter didn't take his clothes off for forty-eight hours and slept in the waiting room, sitting up with odd strangers the whole time.

I had sustained a cerebral hemorrhage. The hemorrhage that killed President Roosevelt was only slightly larger. My hemorrhage, a blot one third the size of the palm of his hand, was apparently at the exact juncture of all the centers of sensation, and the result was that the entire right side of my body—as though one had drawn a dividing line down the middle—was cut off from feeling. The internal organs were apparently not affected. Blood was in the spinal fluid, and this, Walter was told, would be fatal. And that was the first accident.

II

WHILE the insult had seemed sudden and without warning, right there in the Hunter College auditorium with
my performance about to begin and parties following, in
fact it was not as sudden as all that. There had been
warnings, as Dr. Plum says, although I hadn't recognized
them as such.

I had had high blood pressure for some years and was
subject to dreadful nasal hemorrhages, a few of which
required hospital treatment and medical blocking. The
doctors knew all about this and had given me medication
for it, which I took more or less faithfully, and I checked
my blood pressure more or less regularly. But before this
last concert I had been dreadfully slack. I was busy and
had not taken my blood pressure in weeks.

Three times over the past few years I had become
vague, like falling asleep, and lost track of where I was or
what I was doing or what I had just said. But I was not

falling asleep. Twice I was on a lecture platform nearing
the end of an hour-long lecture, the first time without
notes, so that I had to stop, and the second time with
notes, so that I put my finger on the place and mechanically read to the end without knowing whether I had already made the statements or not, or why I was making
them. It was a dreadfully frightening situation. The third
time I was in a rehearsal in Toronto and I was laid flat on
the floor of my dressing room and a doctor was sent for
and he said, "You should be in a hospital with that blood
pressure." But, of course, that was impossible. I had to get
on with the job! I did take the day off, however.

Dr. Fred Plum recalls the hospital events as follows:

> On May 15, 1975, Agnes de Mille went to the edge, looked
> over, and stopped.
>
> The ambulance arrived at The New York Hospital
> about 7:00 P.M. Her life changed at that point. By the
> time she reached us, her right side already lay paralyzed,
> she barely could feel the useless members, and she could
> not see clearly the right side of her world. Her blood pres-
> sure was an alarmingly high 210/115. At least initially she
> remained clearheaded, articulate, and self-controlled, but
> by the standards we later came to know, her spirit was
> uncharacteristically subdued.
>
> Two hours later matters were worse. The right-sided
> sensory loss had become so dense that neither touching
> nor even squeezing of the skin reached Miss de Mille's

conscious awareness. More frightening was the fact that she was getting drowsy and beginning to have trouble thinking of words or speaking clearly, symptoms betraying an enlargement of the damage to involve more humanly vital areas of the intelligent brain.

Medically, the immediately challenging question was not whether she had a stroke but what kind. Sudden paralysis of this type in an older person with known vascular disease or hypertension nearly always reflects an abnormality in the arteries supplying blood to the brain, either a thrombosis (occlusion) or a rupture with hemorrhage.

The accurate diagnosis of certain diseases of the brain, including strokes, has been greatly improved by the development of computerized axial tomography, or the CAT scanner, as the instrument is popularly called. The principle of CAT scanning is relatively simple. Because of their unique chemical compositions, most bodily tissues differ somewhat in their ability to absorb X rays. The technique of CAT scanning consists of circumscribing multiple planes of the head with an X-ray beam that is placed directly opposite a detector on the other side of the skull. A highly advanced computer then calculates the very tiny differences in radio-penetration of the beam across the continuously changing line of tissue which divides the source and the detector of the X rays. Despite the straightforward principle, the engineering, mathematics, and physics of the method is extremely difficult, and its ingenious innovation won a Nobel Prize for its inventor Godfrey N. Hounsfield, and for Allan McCormack, the mathematician whose work made it possible to perform the necessary computations. The resulting picture, or CAT scan (i.e., a computerized axial tomographic scan), reveals an outline of the brain and, to a remarkable degree, the details of many of its internal structures. Most tumors and many other diseases cast shadows of either an increased or decreased density on the CAT image, often with individualistic configurations.

In 1975, when Miss de Mille had her stroke, only a few of Hounsfield's remarkable machines had started operating in New York City. Fortunately The New York Hospital had already been testing the technique and had some five months' experience with its unit when Agnes de Mille became ill. As a result, we were able to picture the interior of her brain within about two hours after her admission.

The CAT results were unequivocal and their implications distressing. The pictures revealed the shadow of a hemorrhage as large as a walnut lying deep in the left hemisphere of the brain, lodged in the structure anatomists call the thalamus (derived from the Greek word meaning inner or hidden chamber, actually used by our classical ancestors to denote the ladies' chamber of a palace). The brain's deep-lying thalamus normally receives and integrates messages coming from the body's sensory receptors and relays information to the cerebral hemispheres, which synthesize the signals into awareness and recognition.

Hypertension is a disorder that, if prolonged and left

untreated, can lethally affect the brain by means of two mechanisms. One occurs insidiously and consists of a slow thickening and wear of the vessel walls resulting from the chronic arterial muscular contraction that must take place to resist the high internal pressure in the artery. The second and more dramatic change is an intermittent, functional one. Episodes of very high systemic blood pressure stimulate the brain arteries to overcontract, producing various local areas of arterial spasm. Adjacent to the spasm tiny cleavages occur in the walls of vessels and small amounts of red blood cells leak from the artery into the tissue. Sustained, untreated hypertension gradually induces thickening and areas of localized weakness in the walls of the smaller arteries of the brain. Medical science still does not know the precise reasons why one of these vessels suddenly gives way, but if one does, a stream of blood, driven by the high arterial blood pressure, gushes into the surrounding soft tissues of the jellylike brain, tearing and compressing vital centers as it penetrates.

Physicians are not completely sure whether it is the areas of spasm or the small leakages that cause the neurological deficits that accompany a very high blood pressure point. But the deficits themselves are well known and consist of episodic spells of drowsiness, confusion, or even fleeting weaknesses and visual loss. Miss de Mille's early warning symptoms were classic medical anticipations indicating that unless she took active measures her hypertension would cause more serious trouble. These dangerous effects of hypertension on the brain have been known for years. What is new in our lifetime and represents one of medicine's great modern discoveries is that the treatment of hypertension at almost any stage reduces the danger of future brain damage. Such treatment can be at least partly effective even when delayed so long that the hypertension has been present for many years.

When those first pictures of her brain were taken, only the next few hours could tell whether the bleeding would stop or whether the leak would flow on until it killed her.

III

THE morning after I was officially pronounced dying I sat up and had breakfast with the remaining hand. The doctors were astonished. It was a good breakfast. And I went to sleep again. From the moment Walter saw me, incoherent but bright-eyed, shoving a boiled egg with my left hand into my lopsided mouth, he took heart, and never again—although there were to be frightful things ahead—did he wholly despair. This was contrary to his habitual way of handling matters, which is black, foreboding, and morbid. Now, however, in twelve hours, he had become an optimist.

"This trouble is temporary," he said.

The doctors weren't so sure.

About noon my son, Jonathan, arrived and my first really vivid recollection is of my two men, side by side, with their faces bent over me, their loving, dear faces, and I knew I was safe.

This had been a long trip for Jonathan. In those hours sitting up and waiting for he knew not what, he confronted for the first time a major loss and the tearing apart of what had been a tight fabric. It was to be the moment of reappraisal and judgment.

I tried to talk to Walter. I could only whisper and rasp. I talked gibberish, but I didn't know that then; although there were no words of English coming out of my mouth, I went on talking and Walter pretended he understood me. "Yes, dear," he said. "Yes, of course I'll do it," presuming, as seemed most likely, that I was giving orders. But how does anyone know? "Wa listen. Wa I groopes? Ye rideargo sutimo? Rev." And then I fell asleep again. And the two stayed there quietly by my bed.

There is a very personal side to this story. I relate it because it has a great bearing on my survival. Our son, Jonathan, and his father had never been close and easy friends. This was a grief to me. But it was a fact and I had to recognize it. However, as those two men bent together, shoulder to shoulder, they began to be friends. Then they went out to dinner and over dinner they resolved many of their troubles. They have been deep friends ever since, deriving great pleasure and joy from their relationship. It started immediately and it happened right there. I don't know how to explain this, but it was so.

And in the afternoon my sister came, hollow-eyed, ashen, exhausted (having gone by mistake to the wrong hospital), in agonizing pain, and she stayed by the bed with Jonathan and his father.

But Walter wanted to be with his son. He had to be. They were reweaving years of ravelled and torn feelings. The two men clung together. She was bitterly hurt, but there was no help for it. In this agony they reacted primitively, as they had to. The men grabbed something in the hospital commissary and dashed back to the bedside. She wept through her dinner alone.

Shared suffering, shared fear make a stronger bond than blood. Pain cracks us wide open and is totally revealing, and this is when we learn whom we really love and this is what we never forget.

My memory is hazy and broken about everything that happened in the next couple of weeks. All was fragmented, partial; part of my brain had drowned. I was also heavily sedated, and as a result there was no proper sequence, no differentiation of personalities, no understanding of pains or disturbances or lacks, just a numb helplessness and the knowledge that I was desperately unable to do what I ought to have been able to do and always had done.

The nurses were a vague assemblage of solicitous anonymity. There were a great number of them, a great number of doctors, a great number of advisors and lookers-on. They blurred.

The nurses had cool, capable hands, freshly starched dresses, low voices. They administered pills and occasionally food, changed my nightdress, changed my sheets. The doctors were professional. I got to know the younger ones better than the heads of staff because I saw them more often and I began to distinguish them by the way they did their hair, which was sometimes extraordinary and sometimes downright unkempt.

The first personality out of all these to focus and clarify was a small, bright-eyed nurse, Miss Maas. She was impressively efficient and always there when I needed her. She became the center of my helplessness and need, I the object and center of her ministrations.

Hubertine Maas ("my father loved beautiful names") was a five-foot-tall Dutch woman, older than the other nurses, with dyed hair and rouge spots on her cheeks. She was assiduously, even brilliantly, careful; by that I mean that she was quiet but alert, a witch with a bandage. In fact, she was better at this than some of the doctors themselves. She showed always great patience and cheeriness and a lovely human enthusiasm for everything except what was tedious and banal. As the days went on, she talked to me a little. She was lonely for her sisters in Holland. Now and then she phoned them. Maas took the day shift, seven to four. She used to have a cup of tea or go lie down when she felt it was safe to leave me, for she suffered dreadfully from stomach trouble and was most of the time in misery. She never spoke of this under any circumstances, but I could tell from her white, pinched face and the accentuated rouge spots. I believe she was in pain almost the whole time.

The evening nurse was Collette Quigley, black-haired, intelligent-faced, Irish, with just a slight, soft lilt to her

speech; very patriotic, very homesick, and extremely interested in what she was doing. She wrote papers on the
research she had been engaged in and she gave them to
me to read later; they were quite extraordinary.

My friend Mary became my guardian and buffer. She
made a great many phone calls—dozens, more than that,
possibly hundreds. She took all the inquiries which were
relayed to her from Walter's office and my telephone exchange. She wrote upwards of four hundred notes of ex-
planation and thanks for flowers and messages. This was
an arduous and onerous service which she undertook
gladly in the interests of friendship and fulfilled without a
word to me until a year later.

We turned to her for everything personal as simply and
directly as we turned to the nurses.

She was not allowed to see me for three days, but she
hung around the halls and waiting rooms just in case. She
told me later that when she had asked Maas how serious
the situation really was, Maas replied, "Mrs. Green, it is
very serious. You see, it is the noblest organ in her body,
her brain, that has been insulted."

Little by little the doctors also made themselves known
to me.

There was Gorham, of course, as reliable as the family
clock. He told the time. He knew. He was there. George
Gorham was an ordinary American, tallish, quiet-voiced,
growing thin of hair, classic of feature, with an American

face and an American body, and not particularly noticeable except that he gave the impression of someone reliable and good, very reliable and very good—a man, in short, someone to count on. Behind the quiet manner was an acute sense of humor. I learned that he was enormously respected in his trade.

Fred Plum, the head neurologist, was more tightly built, slightly smaller, with the astute, intellectually aware manner of an excellent professor or lawyer or a brilliant stockbroker. His manner was quiet, too, but incisive. He noticed everything. Nothing whatever escaped him. He relished everything relishable. He was interested in everything and his word was a command. The hospital staff simply fell away when he appeared. And that reaction had been earned. It is always earned. One gets that sort of respect in only one way—by deserving it. These two I remembered from the start.

But there were many others, great men, neurologists, internists, blood specialists. I didn't bother with names at the beginning, only slowly after weeks.

The big doctors came in twice a day and tried to explain what was going on to one another, or a little to me. The younger residents came in a covey of nine or ten every morning at about eight o'clock and argued quite baldly about all the symptoms and conditions and of what was wrong with me. But they talked their own language, so I understood nothing. They disputed at the foot of my bed and held lively conversations on their way out, huddling, arguing beyond the door, never lowering their voices. It seemed that they were in considerable disagreement. I understood nothing of what they said, but I could understand the tune: bewilderment.

They never addressed a personal word to me or took into account the fact that I was a woman and had some sort of name. Finally, in the second week, I called them back as they were leaving. "Gentlemen?"

Heads turned.

"One thing." A medic stepped back.

"Good morning!"

One doctor grinned sheepishly, but no one spoke and no one laughed. They were already intent on the next case.

But I tantalized them. It was not that I was a good choreographer nor a charming and witty woman but that I had brought a badly damaged toy for them to fix up. My decay seemed to be a curiosity. I became notable for my aberrations. I was catnip. I aroused all the inventiveness and resourcefulness and curiosity of the young craftsmen, and they were as intent on my vascular derangements as I had ever been on choreographic problems when I arrived for rehearsal in the morning. And they were about as gracious.

Walter asked the neurologist, Dr. Fred Plum, if I was out of danger. "No," Plum said. "But she's alive. She's here." And Walter said, "I was told she wouldn't live. I was told there was blood in the spinal canal." And Dr. Plum said, "That need not have been serious." Walter found no suitable comment. "But there were other things quite different. These could be more troublesome. We have to wait and see what develops."

I was taken up with the minutiae of living. Everything was so extraordinarily difficult and so new to perform. Every single act became a contest of skill; and games can be tiring. I did not concern myself with the medical details. There are patients who do, and presume, after a short while, to advise the doctors and to interfere in their conferences. I wanted none of that. I was too much of a pro to know that I must not step out of line. The doctors could not take the time to explain to me what was dangerous or what their plan was. (Did they know?) They got about their business. I watched them at it and I was glad for their expertise, but I did not seek in any way to share it, and even when they tried to explain it to me I resisted. I was reluctant to learn because I didn't think the horrid details would help me to keep my energies where they belonged—on survival. The dreadful possibilities were entirely the doctors' business.

I was alive, but would I recover speech, vision, and mobility? Would I recover memory? The doctors watched and questioned and tested. Twice daily. Sometimes oftener. And then, because I was more or less immobile, my right side quite motionless, there was the dread danger of blood clots forming, and these, of course, could be lethal. I was not warned of any of this, naturally. I did not know at the time whether or not Walter was (he was, it seems), but the doctors knew full well.

In the meantime, I had to get through the days with my petty preoccupations, baby's chores! Now she eats, now she goes to her potty, now she sleeps. But is she growing all the while and toward what do you think? With luck, will she be intelligent?

Five days after the stroke. Mary says she answered the phone to hear, "Hello. It's Agnes." She recalled that my voice sounded low and muffled but perfectly clear and understandable. (I had been unintelligible that late night in the hospital.) I asked her to come to see me that afternoon and to bring Chuck Hollerith.

Mary remembers, "We went along at five, Chuck toting packages of gay cocktail napkins, swizzle sticks, etc., all the accoutrements for a more than adequate bar. We stayed for half an hour or so and when we left I was miserably shaken. In the first place, I could scarcely hear you and I had great difficulty understanding you. Your voice was whispery and hoarse, and the words were slurred. I couldn't figure out what you were talking about. You seemed gay and flip, however, chattering and laughing. Chuck talked and told little gossipy stories and was funny and light, while I sat numbed and dumb. On the way out Chuck said, "I've always thought they should have a bar in the lobby of hospitals."

Mary also recalls seeing me on the following day and two days later, each time at an earlier moment in the day, and each day my voice was stronger and I was easier to understand.

Robert Whitehead, the producer and president of my board, said that when he first came to see me he was surprised at the extent to which my right arm and leg, which of course were under the covers, were immobilized. He said, "In speaking to you the thing that concerned me, because it was dicey, was that you didn't know which way things were going to go. I remember feeling that your reaching for words required an energy that you didn't seem to have at the time, nor did you seem to have the memory for certain words."

I also said words incorrectly. For instance, a word like campaign might come out pancake. I believe this is a common confusion resulting from hemorrhages, but it's damned bewildering for both the speaker and the listener. There were certain simple words in the middle of a sentence that escaped me, and then whoever was with me would try to supply them. Whitehead said, "I remember your frustration and the kind of fury and anger you had. But that seemed very natural to me. The next time I came, there was quite obviously an improvement. At the beginning, however, one wasn't sure in which direction you were going to go. It was scary."

And David Baker: "When I saw you for the first time and remarked that you looked well, which you *did*, you said, 'I feel like an old, empty cardboard box!' I was happy to see the correct forces still at work."

Mary also remembers that I had problems with words. For instance, take this exchange:

"Mary, the next time bring the Mary Janes with you."

Mary Janes? Shoes? Did she need a different kind of shoe?

"Are they in your closet, Agnes?"

Furious. "Of course not in my closet. My God!"

Mary Janes? A woman's name. A person.

"Is it a person?"

"*Of course.*"

"Do I know her?"

Fury. "Of course you know her."

"Is she a member of our company?"

"Oh, Mary!"

Now it was a game. "Is it Jane?" Nod. "Jane Gilman, our lawyer?"

"Of course. I said Jane."

"I'll have her call you, Agnes."

Another time a few days later:

"Mary, the man who cleans up must call me."

My God, she needs a janitor. I wonder why she doesn't ask the nurse.

"What needs cleaning, Agnes?"

"The books, Mary. The books."

Aha. "The company books?"

"Of course." She didn't call me stupid but she looked at me as if I were stupid.

"Our secretary? The company secretary? Chuck Hollerith? I'll ask him to call you."

That noble organ was not going to be so reliable. It was starting to play tricks.

After my sister, Margaret, arrived at the hospital, she had stared at me, her blue eyes clouded with fear, her makeup somehow not on her face but extra, her mouth drawn in pain. There I was, the older sister, the one who had led in all things—now inert. I had been the first to get my hair up, the first to go out dancing—well, she overtook me there in jig time—the first in scholarships, the first to graduate, the first to become known on the stage, the first, the first . . . I was older, you see. I stared back dolefully. "Oh, my," I said very sadly. "Dear Mag." I took her hand in my left one.

The sisters of friends often seemed pallid to us, a second edition, a lesser personality. But Margaret was second to no one. She was younger and in some fields less well known, but she was not lesser. She was beautiful, engaging, and successful. She had many friends, including the Eisenhowers, and she had travelled with them on their official plane, Air Force One. But she knew the leading people in many fields: diplomacy, politics, theater, music, business, moving pictures. Her memory was encyclopedic on all subjects. She was alert, as very few people are, and knowledgeable. And always, on all occasions and at all times of day, she was vivacious and amusing. Her reliable and ready wit and party effervescence made her the life of every drawing room she graced. She was known internationally for this. George Cukor, the moving picture director, said of her, "Oh, she was funny alright, the funniest girl I ever knew. She always amused me." She always amused me, too, even in dire times, even in times when the family was threadbare. She would expend the effort and the trouble to rise to occasions and be sprightly when everyone else flagged, when all hopes drooped—Margaret was funny. She was loyal and candid. And that is perhaps the most unusual gift of all.

She looked up to me because I was the older one. She depended on me because I was stronger, or had been when we started out. I did not fulfill her requirements, being sloppy, untidy, uncareful about money, uncaring about money, uncaring about social fame or even professional success in its more blatant and saleable aspects. Yet she looked up to me.

And shortly before the stroke, there had been her little-girl voice on the phone saying, "Ag, Ag, I'm going to die. It's cancer." She had come to New York. They, the doctors, went inside, the biggest experts in the country. "Riddled," they said, "throughout. No hope." And when the surgeons had finished with her, the chemotherapist moved in and started on the horrible cure, which she had taken like a soldier. It was the way to recover and she intended to recover. It was very cruel and very painful and she was sick to the last cell in her body. But she stood it and was resting from one of those bouts when she had been summoned back to New York for me.

We stared at one another wanly. Mag, my little sister. "Mag, this should have been your show, not mine. You were to die first. Oh Lord, I've done it again." We both giggled.

The doctors asked me constantly if I had any more sensation in my arm or leg. At first they asked me this regularly, at least twice a day. After a while they only asked every few days, and then only every week. I was bored with saying no, but at the same time I wanted them to continue asking, and it was rather dismaying when they stopped.

Due to my inertia, there was grave danger for a blood clot to form. If they gave me medicine to thin my blood so that it would not clot, they ran the imminent risk of starting another hemorrhage. I knew nothing of this, but they told Walter, and this is what they talked about every morning in the hall.

Walter panicked, calling in every specialist he'd heard of. I think he all but buttonholed them in the corridors and on the sidewalks and yanked them in to see me. And, of course, every time one of these august men came and sat on my bed just to say, "You're in good hands," or "I've seen your chart," there'd be a large bill. But Walter was a spendthrift through delirium of fear.

I was to be in the hospital long enough to have the staff on the floor change three times in the regular hospital rotation which ensures the young doctors a fair sampling of all kinds of patients. And the brilliant medic who'd ushered me through the emergency doors left, alas. I probably owe him my life, because he took charge of me immediately and ordered the brain scan. He was a charming young man, although I had trouble making him laugh. He had a thatch of hair like a bird's nest and I imagine he is now well into a brilliant and outstanding career. He was replaced by a young and very gentle resident who managed to make me feel that I was not just Case Whatever but a person whom he rather liked and whom he liked to speak to. This helped. I had eighteen doctors in all, not counting the residents and interns who came around like seasonal schools of fish.

One of the first neurologists to take charge was a young, very able man. One night he and my son found themselves at the elevator door and Jonathan turned to him and said hopefully, "She moved her hand today. That's a good sign." And this doctor said, "Tell me something new, why don't you?" And Jonathan said, "I'm sorry, but I've been told she was dying. I hope she isn't." And then the doctor relaxed slightly and said, "Well, perhaps she isn't. We can hope." Two nights later Walter called up Jonathan at Cambridge at three-thirty in the morning—the first time he had done anything like that— and said, "I'm going to fire him. I don't know how one does this with one of the chiefs of staff, but I'm going to." And Jonathan said, "Alright by me." And so Walter said to Gorham, "We don't want him. He's unsympathetic and hard and we just don't want him." And Gorham said, "All right. Okay."

But then I learned a curious thing: You cannot fire an important doctor. He came in just as regularly and sat and chatted with me comfortably and sent in an enormous bill.

Plum interjected:

> One learns with experiences like this that not all doctors and patients are meant for each other, and that even small efforts at pleasantness can be misinterpreted and devastating to the families of the very sick. This was true between Walter and this neurologist who, I've since learned, has an abundant following of admiring colleagues and adoring patients.

It was at this point that Gorham asked Plum to take charge of the case as neurologist-in-chief.

Anger is a common, natural reaction to the catastrophe of a stroke, Plum tells me.

I relieved myself in fits of irascibility against the nurses. Walter grew outraged with the doctors. Jonathan was short-tempered and snappish with his colleagues. And Margaret was furious with, of all people, me! Why had I driven myself so relentlessly? She had warned me and warned me. Why had I not listened? Why had I persisted in my selfishness, and just when she was so very sick, and in such misery? She had gone to the wrong hospital on the way to me and she blamed Mary for giving her faulty instructions. She was livid with anger against Mary. Rail, rail, rage and rail—we all did it.

The doctors expected this reaction and they paid it not an undue amount of attention. Most of them did, however, show compassion, particularly Gorham. But I truly believe that I suffered the least. That didn't keep me from being bad-tempered. I kicked and spat against small, insensitive things, and against friends who could feel, against friends because they didn't understand me quickly, because I had to rely on them for everything, because I wanted to *do*, and they didn't do, they didn't instantly do, not without explaining. Explaining—Oh God! No shortcuts ever again. I had to be precise, clear, comprehensive. My life was a tangle of explaining—I raged.

I didn't eat all I ordered of the marvelous food (and it was just that—piquant, varied, enticing, but all with little salt, and, so help me, I couldn't tell. The kitchen was on my floor, so the dishes came piping hot). Still, I looked at it with gluttony and all the time I lost weight, fourteen pounds. It was a new experience, like a dream.

My primal concern was, of course, food and water, and next the faces of helpers. And then, as I began to get basic hourly needs straightened out, the extent of the damage to my body and brain, and its manifold symptoms, became evident, unexpected and shocking; there seemed to be so many areas in which I had been besieged and overthrown.

My eyes were affected, not just the right eye, in the terribly hurt side of my face, but my left eye, too. I couldn't see clearly anywhere in the room. I couldn't see people. I kept track of how much I could see by a watercolor on the opposite wall, an autumnal New England landscape. I said to my unfireable doctor one day, quite brightly, "I'm going to be able to see that picture within a week." And he laughed at me and said, "Not a chance." And, quite abashed, I asked, "How long do you think?" And he said, "Maybe with luck in six weeks." It was dreadfully depressing, dreadfully. I couldn't even look at TV at that point. Well, I didn't care. In fact, I cared about very little. I slept.

What worried me agonizingly was that I could not get my touch back. Sometimes I lost track of my right hand completely and had to hunt through the bedclothes to find it. I couldn't feel how long my arm was, or where my hand was in relation to my forearm. I had to feel along the inside of the arm with the left hand until I reached the member. I sensed that I *had* a hand, but it always seemed to be in the middle of the forearm. I actually felt along the bone and into the fingers with astonishment at its length and distance until I came to it, quite surprisingly, a long way off and way down there. I kept being surprised by how long my leg was, how long and far away my foot was. I would feel where my foot ought to be, and where I thought it was, and it was inches, oh, a foot longer, which was startling. And when I raised an arm, I didn't know where it was—before, behind, to the left, to the right. And if I closed my eyes, I didn't know whether it was still up or had moved somewhere else. If I extended an arm, I strained the muscles and tensed them. But the hand always fell to my coverlets and I never knew because I was still making the effort. This is an astonishing experience.

We always know, in normal life, where our hands and feet are. We don't think about them consciously, but we know because there is an unceasing radar playback from every part of the body telling us, "This is there," "This is near," "This is not within reach," "This is painful," "This is comfortable," "This is hot!" "This is soft." We don't have to look and we don't have to be aware, we just know. Now I was without those signals, and I didn't know.

I could feel motor impulses, and in a couple of weeks I learned how to know when I was opening and shutting my hand because I could differentiate the effort and I was generally right in my surmises. But if somebody took my hand and moved it for me and my eyes were shut, I had no idea where it was or if it had been touched at all.

The loss of the sense of touch is not just curious and teasing, something to be remarked upon like a Novo-cained jaw during a tooth operation. It is, as a matter of fact, dangerous and limiting. Touch is with us for a reason, namely, survival, safety and usefulness. And without it we are perhaps more greatly damaged than if we lost our sight or hearing.

Half of me was imprisoned in the other half. The dead side seemed unaccountably heavy, gigantically heavy and restrained with bonds. Cement. Wood. When I rolled in bed and tried to get onto my right, or dead, side, I rolled against a dyke of unfeeling matter which I lacked the strength to go over or rise against. If I rolled to the left, I could not lift the right, not possibly. I lay on my back, un-moving at night for about five months. There were mercifully no bedsores and this is a tribute to the nurses. But I seemed to be incarcerated in a carapace of iron, like a medieval torture suit. It didn't hurt, but I could not get out. Inside were all my viscera pumping, living, moving, contracting, expanding. But if I tried to move or bend or turn my head, there I was, locked in, trapped.

I used to lie awake at night and move my foot. Could I feel my toes? Could I feel *any* toe? Was my foot going up and down and sideways as I thought it was and as I wished and directed? Sometimes I thought I felt, but it might have been the faint, almost imperceptible sound of my nail on the sheet. It might have been, somehow, a brush against the sentient leg and a transfer of signals. Could I feel my hand? What could I do to make my hand feel, to know what it felt? It turned out after hours and hours of experimentation that I could not feel and there was nothing I could do.

Because of the confusion in the sensation centers of my brain, because all of the nerves had become tangled (as though they were ripped like wires out of a telephone exchange and left lying loose and matted, as one doctor explained), I felt lots of strange things that had nothing to do with fact. In a paralyzed arm or leg there is no feeling at all. It is absolutely dead, cut off as though it were no longer a part of the body. Time stops for that limb. Events stop. But I was desensitized, and in what I was experiencing there was a constant tingling in my face and in my arm and leg. This is the classic symptom. Shakespeare speaks of it:

"This apoplexy is, as I take it, a kind of lethargy . . . a kind of sleeping in the blood, a whoreson tingling."*

I felt tinglings, vibrations, numbness or inaccurate awareness; great heat when there was no heat at all, great heat all of the time, so that I looked to see if my body had broken into sweat and found it hadn't, and pain for no adequate reason. For instance, one night I upset a glass of water on my bed tray and in due course the sheets soaked through and the sensation was transferred to my body, but I cried out, frightening my husband half to death, because what had reached me was not the feel of a wet sheet, which everyone, beginning with very little babies, knows about, but pain. I could feel hot water, but not immediately, only after a count of about four and a half, too late to prevent scalding. I felt no cold, and when my hand or the arm was left outside of the covers and I finally happened to retrieve it, it would come in all but frostbitten. I didn't know.

When my foot bumped into something, I felt it in my groin.

There were, in addition, irrational and insane jerkings which I was not aware of. My hand would fly out and encounter, well, whatever there was to encounter. And as for putting a finger out and pointing it at an object . . . out of the question! Nor could I dial the telephone. Of course, holding a pen or the shuttle of a loom was impossible. And training that right hand to do the most primitive bidding was like training a wild animal. Of all the

* *King Henry IV—Part 2*, I, ii

years that I had had it and disciplined it and cared for it and accepted its service there was not a trace, and although I am strongly right-handed and thought right, it was not my hand. It was not anybody's hand. It could have been the hind leg of a donkey.

Inside my mummy of unfeeling insulation, inside my corset, I had to keep alive and intelligent and eager. There was absolutely no other point, no other reason. Make the effort. Don't think. But, of course, there was a seepage of disheartenment from the various unrelenting blocks. It sapped my strength. "Oh," I thought on wakening, "if only I could have two hours of my right hand! Two hours! I could go back." Two hours were not to be given me. I had to go on without the respite. And what I did not realize—and perhaps no one does who has not experienced this, or the doctors who attend them—is the exhaustion that comes from just doing *anything*. Doing any practical chore, any puny, trivial thing costs six times the effort it costs in normal living: sitting up, lifting a fork, riffling through the pages of a magazine. Enormous. One is tired. One sleeps.

IV

ALMOST from the beginning the doctors urged constant teasing efforts toward activity. This was not only to use the wasting muscles and to pull up the fading nerves. This was also to forfend the dreadful consequences of total inactivity. Try to comb your hair. Try to brush your teeth. Try to button your dressing gown. Try to use your right hand with a spoon. Don't be so helpless. You must use your right hand. Try to eat with your right hand. Try to use a knife.

I could not write at all with the right hand. The last intelligible sign I had made was the A for Agnes on Victor's still unsigned contract. I made wild marks with the left, like lassoing butterflies. But at least I could feel with the left. At the beginning no one could read my writing, not even I—no one except Mary.

Up to May 15, as far as it was possible for a woman to be independent, I had been independent. Now, not so. I cared nothing. Let me lie still. Let me be. As far as I was concerned, people could wait on me, serve me, help me in every way. I summoned a nurse to scratch my face. Heavens! I could have put out my eye if I tried scratching my own face.

The doctors kept questioning: Is there any more sensation in the hand? in the foot? in the leg? Did you know that I'd been sticking a pin in your arm all the time I was talking? Do you feel any internal pain? Any in the abdomen? in the chest? in the arms—either arm, right or left— no matter how small? Any pains? You must not ignore this.

At the very beginning I had toyed with the idea that maybe I'd better commit suicide. I didn't have the idea strongly enough to make any plans or even consider how I could encompass the act. But it seemed the chivalrous thing to do. It was my fault. I hadn't taken care of myself. I hadn't taken my medicine faithfully. Henceforth to be an absolute lump, a burden to my family, a drain on my husband—isn't suicide what was sporting? To slip away and give freedom to my beloved. But I didn't want to. I wasn't ready. I have the idea that if one intends to commit suicide, one had better want to. I didn't.

What else did I dare think about? Not so very much. Nothing profound. I didn't kick against fate. The fact was, I had had a long and vigorous life. While I had had my body I had used it, God knows. I was lucky to have had it full of health and effectiveness as long as I had. This accident was drastic, but it was not outside the laws of life or humanity. I did not say, "Why me?" because the answer was so patently clear: "Why not me?" I knew I was facing possible extinction, but I trusted not just yet.

I may not have railed against fate, nor cursed my lot, nor imprecated the Almighty. Maybe not. I reserved my attacks for where they could be felt. My spitting impatience, my frenzied, daily exasperation was spent not on impersonal forces but on the kind vulnerabilities of loving friends who could be hurt. The organ in my head may possibly have been noble, but the organ in my breast was not.

Friends who called me two weeks or so after the incident remember clearly my fury, my baffled anger, like a trapped animal not understanding what had happened and how to escape.

But in the meantime there was love—and don't ever forget that.

Fred Plum comments on this period:

The morning after the stroke brought the realization that at least for the time being the worst had passed. One could find no evidence of new neurological losses and Miss de Mille's speech, although still halting and disjointed, at least made some sense. More important, she *looked* better, with that hardly-to-be-defined difference in color, visage and spirit that one finds so easy to recognize yet so difficult to explain in scientific terms.

From then on, for the next month, gradual improvement was the rule. Within days she talked as clearly as ever,

betraying an astonishing and at times disquieting understanding of both the contributions and sometimes insensitive limitations of the medical ritual. The nurses began
immediately to move her about in bed, patiently flexing
and extending each limb, trying to prevent the potential
dangers of immobility to her veins, skin, muscles and
joints. Two or three days later she started active physical
therapy, at first to assure her that her still normal limbs
retained their strength, then to reclaim whatever motion
possible from the paralyzed parts. For those first four
weeks after the hemorrhage, as the CAT shadow of the
hemorrhage at first shrank and then disappeared, gradual
recovery followed. At least for the time being, the climb
was all back towards safety.

I tackled my strange, maimed existence. Have you ever
run a three-legged hobble race? Would you like to try to
keep running in this fashion for the rest of your life? How
about one leg?

The doctors continued to urge effort.

First I was told that I would try hand therapy. A
charming young woman, quite pregnant and with the
manner of forget-me-nots and teddy bears, came to my
bedside with a little handloom and showed me how to
take the shuttle in my right hand and slide it to the left. I
dropped the whole thing on the floor. She picked it up patiently and said, "Throw it right back now." So I shot it
from left to right with alacrity. And then she said, "And
now try from right to left with the right hand." And I

threw it back onto the floor. This went on with no variance for fifteen minutes. Finally I said, "I don't think this is getting us anywhere." She said, "Oh, I think you're doing just wonderfully." And then she said, "What do you like, red or blue? Or shall we have green here?" And I said, "I don't care, really. I can't use the hand." And she said, "We must persist. We will go through the threads very nicely after a while." In brief, I found her intolerable. But every day I had to do one hour of that.

At the conclusion of one early session, my young teacher, drunk on dreams of glory, attempted to walk me around the room, staggeringly, perilously, and she decided to put me back into bed on the unfamiliar side. I begged not, but she was stubbornly optimistic and she propped me on the edge of the bed and started to get me in and I fell through her arms. I was saved by Maas, who, entering my den, took a flying tackle to support my weight. Somehow, together they got me into bed and then Maas turned on the young woman teacher and scolded her bitterly. The girl was humiliated because frightened and she apologized. And, of course, I was scared speechless.

"Don't fall. Don't ever fall," the doctors had warned. "If you give your brain another hard knock, if you have another cerebral accident, it will be a great pity. It will be, in fact, extremely dangerous, so take every precaution and don't get bumped. You're going to bruise extremely easily."

The specialist in rehabilitation medicine who had me in

her charge, Caroline McCagg, a handsome, slim, smart young woman who had been an undergraduate at Sarah Lawrence when I was a trustee, came to see me and said, "You really were rather rough with the hand therapist."

And I said, "I can't stand her. She baby talks. I find it humiliating. What has happened to me is grave. (McCagg shut her mouth tight. It was indeed.) And I'm a pro. Treat me seriously."

I think it was decided at this juncture that all of the hand therapists would rather not have me as a student—or patient. I was extremely caustic. And why not? I had taken lessons from some of the greatest teachers in the world and I was disciplined and resented being talked to like a four-year-old child. Of course, I now had the body of a three-year-old and the brain of one aged two, but my critical faculties were not those of a three-year-old and I was bitterly resistant to lollypops. So they decided not to have me as a solo student anymore. Thereafter I was to take potluck in therapists. They probably drew lots to see who could escape me.

What they did not explain to me then, but what Dr. McCagg clarified much, much later was the specific reason for all this!

"Occupational therapy tries to incorporate exercises into functional movements to reinforce visual, tactile, and motor stimuli, which can then be applied to basic activities. For example, with weaving, the passing of the shuttle back and forth helps a patient learn how to go from the normal to the involved side and back again. Getting the sense of how to pick up cues from the uninvolved side is basic to starting feeding, dressing or just plain following a line across a page."

This is interesting, clear, reasonable. I could have agreed to this quite simply. But they didn't explain, and none of this excuses the regrettable style of that silly girl.

Hitherto I had seen very few of the other patients in the hospital because I had been closeted in my room except when taken down the halls on a stretcher for one X ray or another. I saw then only other stretchers, or I saw the pasty-faced, old, broken, shambling figures trundling on wheeled rods their bizarre insignia, bottles of drip medicine—all of them listless or bad-tempered, in various states of disarray. They looked dispirited. There is nothing dashing or debonair about extremely sick patients, and I was in a ward of extremely sick and forlorn people.

But on the whole I liked the meeting and passing of the strange, nomadic population, the staring in at other people's doors where depressed-looking visitors and families tried to chatter with prone inhabitants over the snatches of TV music coming through the cracks and glimpses of soap operas over the tops of screens.

Now, in the hand-therapy class, I saw the contents of all the rooms, debouched and wheeled into view.

And there we all were.

The therapy room was quiet. Many could not speak at all. Many spoke garbled language. All were intent and absorbed in what they were doing. Only the voices of the attendants could be heard, very soft and very patient, explaining, encouraging, guarding.

The classroom was a grim sight, but one got used to it as with everything: It seemed like something out of Breughel. For here were the maimed, the twisted, the gnarled, the halt, the speechless, the sightless. All there. All trying, in their little, gnomelike, inefficient, grisly ways, to do something, if not useful or pretty, at least sensible. And all, like hurt bugs or worms, failing dreadfully with their lost or mangled members, doing all those footling, silly things, trying to relearn what had been learned painstakingly in infancy: how to hold a pencil, how to handle a needle, how to string beads. But now not with hands. With hooves, rather, with claws, with talons, like the men in the uranium laboratories who work with great steel fingers through steel and rubber partitions, watching what they do through goggles. Our hands were not our hands. Our arms were not our arms. We used extensions. But we never could take off the goggles and masks; we never put down the extensions. The work requires iron discipline, because one hopes to be useful and effective, because, although the heart of life lies behind and one faces a diminishing time with waning strength, one just prays and hopes to be less of a burden to one's daughter-in-law. There was only one single thing that was ours: the determination to do what we wished to do, no matter how awkward, how maimed, how slow. What one saw everywhere was the steady intent standing out above all circumstances: I WILL.

"I will" became the instinctive force of every waking moment, unconscious, troubled. I held on to this impulse as to breath itself. When a doubt assailed me, I simply stopped the doubt. I'd learned to do this in my work. I knew yielding to doubt was very dangerous. Not for one minute, not for three minutes must you allow yourself to get lost in this miasma. If you felt discouraged, stop. Think only of how to cope. Only. And if you're tired, rest. Go to sleep. I slept sixteen hours a day. Of course I was very heavily sedated. But I was also husbanding whatever life impulse was left. I guarded it like the secrets of state. I guarded it like a threatened child. Don't give way, not for one minute, because you will be lost if you start that.

I didn't cry once, except when my French cook came to visit me with garden roses and exasperated me to absolute impotence with claims. "Bijou," my husband called her. The dispute was about money, naturally. She left to bide her time, which the French call *attendre l'heure.*

"*Pauvre* Mme. Prudel!"

It is generally assumed (by those who don't know) that life in the hospital must be dull. This I found out is not so. If one is not in pain—and I was not—it can be rather charming. And if one is alert—and now I was for two or three hours every day—it can be interesting. Certainly bustling.

The day began with cleaning up and feeding and then the routine visits of the doctors. The morning was taken up with X rays or therapy. After lunch came the visitors.

There are those people who know how to visit the very sick and those who don't. Visiting is an art. The chief virtue should be brevity, the second sensitivity, and the third, or perhaps the fifth, sympathy. Everyone is sympathetic, but not many people know how to extend it or in what degree or, certainly, to what lengths. When I was with visitors, I subjected myself to their entertainment as long as I liked and then the first minute it began to pall I closed my eyes, leaned my head back and said, "I don't think I can go on." With some I didn't have to say this, not with my close friends. With some I did. A cheery conversation with the very depleted is not a prolonged interrogation, although it is commonly supposed so. Also, long, garrulous anecdotes about unrelated matters in no way connected are fatiguing, as they are to everybody. But the weak have no refuge. In extremes one shuts one's eyes and says, "Find a nurse." One puts back one's head. (One has to do so many tiring things the doctors constrain one to do. There's strength enough for that and nothing else.) There are those who hold salons, go through the whiskey and perform on their own personalities. A famous writer spent two and a half hours talking about himself, drinking and discussing his current work. I was ashen when he left the room. He didn't notice, of course. "I'll be back next week," he said comfortingly, "with my new manuscript."

There is one sovereign remedy for all of this: the absolute prohibition of visitors from the sick room. But then, of course, one invites despair.

Around six or seven, guests were sent packing immediately, relatives or no.

It was then that Dr. Plum used to sit with me and talk about books, about gardening, about farming, about music—rarely about my ailments. But he was there and I made a complete report to him of every tiny episode. This he insisted on.

"Have you had any pains in your chest? Are there any pains in the abdomen? Do you have pains in the arms? Any kind of pain? Any slight pain?"

I kept shaking my head, "No, no."

"Let me know the minute you have any pains, no matter how slight, no matter how inconsequential, immediately."

"Sure I will; seems silly."

"Just do that."

He came every evening and sometimes I thought, "Oh, I wish he'd come sooner or later. It's just the time for the news." That's when he came and sat down cozily and chatted. And I thought, vain as I was, that he was charmed by my personality and my humor. In fact, he was watching my eyes, he was watching my breathing, he was watching the way I moved my hand, the way I moved my body. He was gauging my condition and he was adjusting what he would say to what he saw. I was on the knife-edge of existence and I stayed there for weeks as he watched. And the others hovered near the door, together with the two faithful nurses. And these women brought me trays of letters or flowers and watched every symptom, every indication. And I imagine, although I don't know, that emergency equipment was standing very close in the hall. I don't know. I think Walter did.

It was the art of Fred Plum, more perhaps than the medical knowledge, that guided him in this period through the ensuing dreadful days. He said very much later, after the danger of immediate death had passed, "I wanted to say, 'Stay as you are. Don't change in any way at all, don't make a move,' but I didn't dare say that."

Dr. McCagg used to come despite my hard usage of her therapy teachers. Dr. Gorham did not come for three weeks. He had gone away on his summer vacation. It was summer, you see, June; the hospital sometimes made me forget, but it was.

When Dr. Plum left each day, it was evening. And at seven-thirty, which was the end of my day and guests and doctors, my husband came. I begged him to be the last so that he could kiss me good-night, and he only missed two evenings in the whole summer.

The late evening hours were very pleasant, the curtains stirring in the night air, the slow summer sun dying ruddily off where I couldn't see it, throwing warm, antique light over our part of New York, the corner of the river that I could see shining sapphire and reflecting sky colors, with the big boats and barges still plying; and then real dusk and the city lights blooming through; the pleasant, busy hospital noises taking over. Late at night, well, eight-thirty (but that was late for me because dinner was at five-thirty) Quigley, my nurse, would say, "Would you like a chocolate malted?" Oh, heaven! Hitherto absolutely forbidden. And she would bring me one. And she'd have something. And we'd simply sit and smack our lips and grin at each other. We sat in the dusk with the room light off and the corridor light making patterns on the floor and the friendly, subdued but busy noises of the busy people outside walking silently, talking loudly, but not too loudly. And absolutely no radio sounds except from the patients' rooms—you could ask them to shut the door if you wanted—and the electric summons to the doctors. Even these stopped at eleven. It was hot, I suppose, because we were in midsummer and no air conditioning was allowed in the hospital, but I was high up and there was always a breeze of sorts. And I lay with only a light sheet across me, watching the night patterns on the ceiling change and sway, and listening to the gradual diminishing of the bustling noises, the hurrying of rubbered feet, the sound of rubber wheels as a stretcher went by, instructions given and understood, but not by me. Bells, the leaving of all guests.

Across the hall came the voice of a man in shocking duress. "Don't! Don't do it! Don't hit me! Don't. Not again! Oh, help! Oh, come to me. Don't do it!" This went on for about two hours every evening and, I suppose, during the day, but there were then enough other sounds to mask the horror.

"What is the matter with that poor soul?" I asked my nurse.

"He was mugged."

"Can't somebody ease his pain? Can't somebody stop his terrors?"

"Oh," said the nurse, "he doesn't feel anything and he doesn't know anything. His brain is damaged."

"Don't do it! Don't do it! Help! Don't hit me!"

And then, sometimes, the little rubbered feet running and breathless voices and the sound of the wheels on a stretcher. And then the quiet again and it was night, the almost soundless tread of the inspecting nurses and the hooded light. "You can't sleep? You want something? Can I get you anything?" Night.

V

I COULD not sit around watching for troubling symptoms that I didn't understand or even know about. That was not my métier. I got on with what I could do and let the others do the policing.

About a month after I arrived, as I began to settle into the hospital routine, I sent for my manuscript. It was not a manuscript of a book I was really working on. It was a manuscript from a while back I thought I might work on, an odd jumble of papers, really. Mary brought them to me, armfuls of them. (They eventually became a book, *Where the Wings Grow*.) I could only read three or four pages at a time, but some of it seemed rather pleasant to me, and it reminded me of beneficent things: my youth, my parents, the woods of my childhood. But I could only write a few words at a time.

And the great difficulty was not in thinking or even doing slow, left-handed writing, but in handling the papers. The papers slipped. The papers fell to the floor. The papers got lost in my bed. Paragraphs got lost. I could face the loss of my leg because that was serious, that was dignified, but the loss of a goddamned paragraph, that was maddening! I couldn't turn forward or back in the manuscript without scattering everything all over the bed. I couldn't hold the papers up to examine them, not more than one at a time. The papers exhausted me, and every time I wanted the manuscript brought to me or picked up I had to send for my nurse.

"Now, please, put that chapter there and let me see the next one. No, not that. This. No, this." The handling of the papers defeated me. And then there were pencils which got lost or fell. And there were scissors. I made up my mind that I would never use the scissors with my left hand. I had to insert my right fingers into the scissor eyes mechanically with my left hand, and if I took my attention off the blades they slipped and I found myself sawing at the air with a loose thumb. Never mind. Put the thumb back. Five times reinserting the wayward thumb in cutting across one page. Six times. Put it back. Try again. Drop them. Ah, there. They've fallen to the floor. Send for the nurse. Put it back. Try again.

But the pages, when I set them aside, stood on a special table covered with a towel, and they represented the far shore. They represented safety. This was reassurance. This was tomorrow. A goal. They were there, banked for me. The only future I had. I let my eyes rest on them when I couldn't handle them. I thought of them in the night and they were a promise. It is not enough to live in "now" as we have been told. We have to surmise "tomorrow." I imagine ths is the difference between humans and animals. Take away tomorrow and the spirit is truncated.

I had not given myself a time schedule to meet. I don't like to do that with any difficult task, and this one was pretty hard. But I thought that in a month I would be up and about, certainly. Not well, but able to negotiate and get from place to place. I could do nothing like this, it turned out: I couldn't understand. Still, it was a month I had been in the hospital, four weeks.

Jonathan says I kept probing in every conversation with him.

"Will I begin lecturing in six months? Eight? Can I take a theater job in a year? How soon?"

He didn't know. The question he kept asking was, "Will she live?"

But I was still alive and I was keeping interested and I was improving in small ways, with a certain amount of feeling coming back into my face. My eyes were better. My mouth had pulled back into shape. I no longer drooled. My speech was more or less clear, although far from glib, my voice still low and clouded. I could follow a line to the end and go to the next. The sensitivity in the hand and foot had not altered one jot, but the mobility of the members was stronger. The ataxia, that is, the shaking and dancing of the muscles of both the leg and arm, was crazy and drove me quite beyond control. When I was with company I held onto my right hand with my left lest I do something grotesque and disturbing.

One month, the longest time I had ever been sick; the longest time I had been unable to do what I wanted to do and intended to do. But I had survived the hiatus in my life.

The one-month date corresponded with the thirty-second anniversary of our wedding. Walter said he would give me a party, something he had never before done.

And so now we would celebrate, first, the anniversary and then, incidentally, the fact that I was alive and going to be well shortly.

Whenever we could, we have always made a good thing of our anniversary parties. They have been very festive. We've had them all over the world and we've had very joyous ones. The twenty-fifth anniversary was a tremendous party at Oliver Smith's house in Brooklyn Heights, and everybody wonderful that we loved came. Gwendolyn Killebrew, Jerome Hines, Cesare Valletti and Jan Peerce sang part of an opera Walter had composed when he was twenty-one and hadn't heard since, and Isaac Stern played our wedding march. Oh, it was delicious!

"I wanted this to be a surprise," said Walter, "but the doctors forbade me to give you a party. They said you had had a surprise this summer."

However, he didn't tell me the guest list. I was just told that there was going to be a party and that I was to have my supper promptly at five o'clock and to eat lightly, which I did. And then at six o'clock Mary Green came in and brought my beautiful Benares pink silk dress and jewels to match and braided my hair hospital-style, but with ribbons. And she made me up. And then I was tucked into my chair and Walter rolled me down the hall to the corner dining room, which is used for fêtes and board meetings. And there were my friends, all my beloveds, all Walter could reach, come from all over. There was champagne and flowers and very attractive food—not a real meal, just good things to eat with champagne, and I was allowed a thimbleful of that. We could see the river sparkling in the afternoon light, and above the skyline a live, roseate and effulgent glow, intense with imminent sunset, small clouds ballooning up and lively with light. The whole landscape was bathed in an amber glow, very eighteenth century. The river scene reminded me of Canaletto paintings of London, and all about us stood the great, monumental buildings glowing in the sunset. And inside, our friends' faces, kind in the candlelight. Mary Green had lit her mother's silver candlesticks.

The celebration was topped by the hospital's present, a great big beautiful wedding cake, very rich and delicious. (The wedding cake Walter and Jonathan had brought was later given to the nurses.) And I knew that my friends and Walter were glad that I was alive, glad for me, glad for Walter. Glad for what I was beginning to be able to do. And there was happiness there because I was going to live. And we had toasts, many of them. They did. I had only a thimbleful of the champagne!

Robert Whitehead remembers it as "a lovely party, adorable. We were all very happy. There was a spirit among us of congratulation and jubilation. It was triumphant. We had together done something successful."

At eight o'clock I found myself in bed, tucked quietly away. Walter leaned over the pillow.

"I'm going to live," I whispered. "I'm going to make it. I'll be out of here soon."

And he whispered back, "I never doubted it. You will be, very soon." And he kissed me good-night and shepherded the others away to dinner. The nurse turned out the light and patted the sheet into place and said in her neat, soft way, almost shyly, precisely and dearly, "All my hearty congratulations. Go to sleep now."

I was asleep. I was safe. I was going to live. I was gathered up and protected.

"Don't do it! Don't hit again! Don't!"

I was asleep.

VI

THE next day life, with its exercises and endeavors, resumed and the doctors, for some inexplicable reason, seemed to go into higher gear. They ordered all the old tests over again. Why, in God's name, why?

When one lists what I did it seems like a gentle life, habitual and fitted with daily, routine chores. But the strenuousness of those chores, the effort involved, was enormous. For instance, the repetition of those tests I had had when entering the hospital to see how much improvement there was. They gave me the brain scan over again in the monster that the intern with the wonderful birdthatch hair had ordered upon my sorry arrival on May 15. I could remember scarcely any of that experience because I had been all but moribund then. The visit back later I do remember.

In appearance the camera was like a great X-ray machine, the headpiece like a gigantic hair dryer in a shampoo parlor, and there is a kind of bathing cap that fits over the skull. I believe this is insulated in some way and also cooled, I'm not sure by what. And that is so the brains or the machine will not fry. I can't remember which. The machine takes several thousand pictures in the space of forty-five minutes and the exercise went on for nearly an hour. Every nine minutes or so they stopped the machine and came back in the room where they had sealed me to tell me that it wouldn't be long now and to find out if I were alive and things like that. There had been, of course, the grand question of whether or not I would be on the first go around. But the second seemed slickly easy and there wasn't a trace of the clot, which was the thing most feared. The original dot had all been absorbed, so that was nice. And then they started on all the chest X rays and did those.

What they found they kept to themselves. I never knew, but I fumed to get out of that hot hospital, to get up to the country, to get away.

After that I continued the therapy I feared and the therapy I despised. The despised you know about. I started a placemat, greenery, yallerly, under the auspices of a classically minded and exacting redhead whom I liked very much.

The feared was just the same: challenging. I had a walker and I was told to stand up in it. There were two nurses for that, one on each side. Well, I stood up. I stood on the left leg and the right dead creature that I was attached to did something or other to drag me down and throw me on the floor. And the nurses supported the inert lump and then put it back into bed. Then I was dispatched to a proper all-body, stand-up therapy class.

In the morning I was helped onto a mat and made to use my legs while lying on my back. I couldn't recognize my right leg, which had been the guiding leg, of course, because I am right-handed. I couldn't do a bicycle motion. I couldn't point my toe. I couldn't hold my leg still. It wavered and dropped, flopping from side to side. It didn't matter what I wanted. I couldn't do it. Then somehow they turned me over on my stomach and they tried to bend my right knee and I screamed with pain, and this was real pain.

"We're only flexing your right knee."

"My God, don't ever do that again," I shrieked. And then they asked me to get up on all fours. That I could just possibly manage. And then they asked me to put all my weight on my left knee and left hand and lift the others, the useless arm and the useless right leg. Well, I could sort of do that for one and a half seconds. And then Gerry Donato, my therapist, who really was pressing me (through ambition, pride and affection), asked me to put all my weight on the right side and lift the left leg and, of course, I fell hard on my chin. Maas gathered me up and took me back home in the chair.

I began the real exercises, the exercises that were not boring, like the hand therapy, but frightening. I stood between the double bars, one hand on each, which was comfortable and felt safe, except that the right hand was no use and kept falling off. And I was encouraged to stand and then walk. It was terrifying. The left leg was fairly steady, although it had been idle for some weeks. The left hand was fairly reliable. But the right half of the body was nothing but an encumbrance and weight. I could not get my balance, and I could never know when I had my balance, because at this point I did not even feel the weight of my foot on the ground, so that when I put my right foot forward I didn't know whether my weight was on it or not on it, and I had to watch it every second because there was a spastic inclination to curl the foot inward. Several times I turned the foot over and put my weight on the side carelessly, nearly breaking the ankle. Every time I put the right foot out, I trusted the whole of the rest of the mechanism—my head and my teeth and my eyes and my heart and my viscera—to what? This was frightening.

I have always been very timid physically, unusual and unworthy for a dancer. Dancers are brave. Dancers launch themselves into the air. Dancers throw themselves into the arms of their partners. Dancers balance high up, held aloft, holding their spines straight and trusting their partners to catch them if the whole edifice comes crashing down, unlike me, who had not the physical bravura. I didn't trust. I didn't hold straight. I was a snivelling acrobat. Now I was up against a real problem. Walking, even holding on with the left hand, was very hard and very daring, even walking while watching the mirror was simply trusting my sentient being to absolute unknown

forces and unknown balances. I swung out over an abyss.
It was me and gravity, with no tangible relationship. I
quailed.

Remember that if I fell, I fell like a log, probably on my
face and certainly on my head. The left hand was busy
clutching, clutching something, a stick or a chair or an
arm or the air. The right hand was incapable of supporting
my weight or pushing. It turned over spastically, so I always exposed the weak back of the wrist and it rendered
me totally unable to defend myself. I fell on my face,
straight, through gravity, on the nose and mouth. I was
craven alright, a real coward, but I didn't like to fall raw,
peeled. Not on the nose and mouth.

I used to measure the distance to the end of the barre,
where I was permitted to turn around and come back:
"Two more feet. One more foot, turn. Fifteen feet. Ten
feet . . ." And the blessed relief, the chair waiting and
my darling Maas with her quiet hands.

And it wasn't as though I felt nothing. I just felt nothing helpful. It's as though my leg had been amputated at
the groin and then soldered together with a thick layer of
bread crumbs. "Graham crackers," I explained to Gerry.
They grated and crunched (not audibly) and they tin-
gled. And then came the leg. The weight on the foot produced sensations—tingling, not reassuring. These sensations would normally have preceded real pain, as in a
sprained ankle. There was, however, no real pain, only
extreme apprehension, because I didn't know what was
happening; a tremendous sense of weakness and peril. In

fact, the hour up in the exercise room was a test of courage. I just had to get through it and I had to try to do what they asked me to do, trusting that they would not let me fall, that they would sustain me, that they would not let my right arm crumple, which it often did.

One can endure almost any pain one understands. A broken ankle? Well, one doesn't put weight on it. That's simple. But this! What was this? One put weight on it. It didn't get better. It didn't get worse.

Many people have said, "How difficult for you! How much more difficult than for anyone else! How cruel because you are a dancer!" This, of course, is nonsense. The experience is difficult. It's final and it's lasting. But it's easier precisely because I was a dancer. I have submitted to physical discipline the whole of my life. I have learned to obey.

I had learned to mind my p's and q's at the barre when I was thirteen, but before that at my mother's knee when I was three. She taught me to sew. As soon as my fingers were able to manage a threaded steel spike, I was put to work on hems, seams, double seams, French fells, plackets, buttonholes (most men and even a majority of women will not know what I am talking about these days), and I became a good seamstress and a fine amateur embroiderer. And this took time, hours of it, summers of it. We never sat idle in our house. We never sat still. Someone read or people chatted, but we never sat still. And we had to sew correctly or embroider neatly and keep our threads in order. And this was time and trouble. My grandmother, whom I never knew but who seems to have had very sound ideas, used to say, "Sewn with the red blood of time." And now it was all paying off for me because I did not quail before the hours and hours that lay ahead in learning to do what I had done very merrily in infancy. To walk, for instance.

I learned patience that the ordinary nondancer never experiences. It takes the human being roughly two years to learn to walk, three years to learn to say words in fluent sentences and five or six years to learn to use the hands intelligently. I had to start all over again. If it took two years to learn to walk, I would have to spend two years. This did not confound me. It was an exercise that had to be done. I had learned to get on my points and do fouetté pirouettes. That took roughly twelve years. That took my youth. I had learned to play the piano quite well. That took twelve to fourteen years of two hours a day of concentrated application.

I just must not hurry or expect to hurry. And little by little I learned. Little by little, very, very slowly.

I became the mascot of the therapy department because I obeyed instructions, as I'd been taught all my life to do, and because I was so sick and hurt.

The faculty of the therapy rooms were young, vigorous girls, like gymnasium teachers, except that they were highly trained and were really feminine and remarkably patient. There were a few men, in particular one beautiful, six-foot-two stalwart man named Edward, who, although as strong as a lion, had probably the worst posture of any young man I've ever seen. I chivvied him and scolded him and remonstrated about his stance, and he listened attentively and we practiced corrections in front of a mirror and he never improved. But he brought me a piece of his birthday cake.

My own particular teacher, Gerry, of the dark curls and laughing eyes, drove me hard, so hard she had me panting with effort and terror. And when she went away on vacation I went to other therapists and improved, I thought. But she came back and made it very clear how disappointed she was with my progress and with the fact that I only gave a few minutes every day to practicing, whereas I should have practiced three times a day, hard. She was so demanding that Dr. Gorham finally had to call her off and tell her there were other things to be considered besides the recovery of my walk. She was never reconciled to that compromise. It was wasteful and dreadful and she was a perfectionist. I loved this in her.

Dr. McCagg explained to me the point of view of the therapist:

"Every patient feels that therapists are Simon Legrees in disguise as pretty, young, exuberant girls. I think that the patient would just as soon be left alone. After all, when you're sick you feel you should rest! On the other hand, therapists are usually young and vigorous and have no awareness of how very sick patients can be. I constantly have to try to rein in their enthusiasm. They are also brainwashed that they mustn't allow patients to 'manipulate' or 'weasel out' of work, etc., etc., and when they are insecure they don't know how to judge whether they are not reaching their goal because they aren't doing the right thing. I have noticed that when this happens they start to lean on patients unfairly."

One very strange phenomenon was that every time I made a physical effort, or indulged in any physical exercises at all, the right side of my face and the mouth began to itch. There was no mark on the skin, no welt or blemish, but the itching persisted until I had stopped exercising. It was not intolerable, but it was maddening—like a finely drawn net of hair across the flesh, or insects walking very delicately over and back, not biting, just travelling. And it was awkward because I had to scratch with the left hand, which was generally occupied with the walker or barre. I dared not scratch with the right hand. I feared for my eyes. And I had prolonged sneezing attacks whenever I exercised. These drove my friends crazy.

Day by day, week by week, I did recover. My sight came back fully. I began to see the whole picture on the opposite wall, the bottom as well as the top, the right corner as well as the left, and it turned out to be what I had suspected, absolutely without merit. In another week I could see the thing in its entirety easily, and the picture was really inexcusable.

But I'd gotten my sight back. It was achieved. I still

couldn't read. I couldn't read at all for five weeks, and then I had great trouble in making my eyes go from line to line of the printed text. They tired unreasonably soon and of course I couldn't hold a book. It had to be propped on the bed table.

VII

"CARNATION, lily, lily, rose." So wrote John Singer Sargent and went off and painted it, an absolutely delicious picture of children decorating Japanese lanterns by candlelight in a summer garden.

Carnation, lily, anemones in spring; "Anemones all over" quoted Will Holt; lilies of the valley, violets, lilies of all kinds, squill, dogtooth violets, hyacinths, camellias, azaleas, roses, roses and carnations; and now, in June, peonies, delphiniums, roses, tiger lilies, mixed and wreathed by master hands; late June, zinnias, a farm basket of garden jollity, musky-smelling. "This will pass, don't be frightened," wrote the sender, Max Rudolph, who had had a bad stroke and was on a podium conducting within ten months. "It's bad now but it passes." Phlox, roses, moss roses, fat, dear, quaint, evocative of my mother's garden, chrysanthemums, wrong season, acrid and earth-smelling but wrong season, alien to the time of the June roses; the exotic Australian and African protea, all alien but curious.

"Nurses, have you kept the cards and written on the backs the names of the flowers?" I tried to write "roses" with my left hand.

And the pillows; the sweet, white, frilly comforts, the pretty things I'd always coveted and not had the money to buy. They came bouncing in, in tissue paper, in ribbons, foaming with ruffles and with fine embroideries, maiden pretties. The hospital sheets were pure, sterile, plain as a prayer, and the plain bed skirts, for convenience of course. I wore the hospital shirt but I spread the lovelies on my bed, the gossamer jackets, the illusive robes.

"Don't do it. Don't hit me."

"Don't mind him. He's off his head."

"May I come in? I'm the office manager. I've come to check if . . . What lovely flowers!"

"I'm the head of the nursing staff. I allot the nurses. Have they worked out? Well, that's par. If ever you want someone special, speak to me. I try to keep the really good ones for where they're needed. I choose carefully."

"May I come in? I'm a patient down the hall. You don't know me. I'm going home. I'm actually going home. They're releasing me. I had to go to every room in this wing and tell them. I'm going home. Good-bye. Good luck."

"Don't mind the screams. He's . . ."

"But isn't the terror as real as though he understood?"

"Help! Come to me!" Where was the voice? Silence. Did he die?

"No. They took him away. Bad for other patients."

"Yes."

If I had the use of my thumbs I'd give up my foot. If I had part of my right hand . . .

"Do you expect me to pick this up?" This from a very beautiful floor nurse, a Panamanian, who stares, arms akimbo, at some papers on the floor.

"Well, I'm not here to pick up the mess your friends make. Who do they think they are? How does a visitor get off throwing papers around the floor for me to pick up?" She sullenly picks up one green flower paper.

"Put that down," I order, rather more sharply than usual. "Put that right back on the floor. The person who threw it down was Dr. James Semans, who is the head of the hospital in Durham, North Carolina. I'm sure he wouldn't want his waste to be handled by anyone except his peers. I will ask Dr. Plum and Dr. Gorham to clean the floor. You may watch." Our relationship deteriorates. Her gaze is pure hatred. Mine is pretty hating, too.

But she is as beautiful as a noon day in a forest and, what's more, when she is with her colleagues in the corridor her laughing is a peal like fresh water.

"May I come in? I'm on the staff. I'm a liaison officer between patient and administration. Patients don't know their rights and sometimes management doesn't. Right now we're trying to get rid of some Gypsies. One is very sick. He can stay. Nineteen others are not sick but watching. They can't. They camp all over the floor and corridors, bring their own bedding, cook on Sternos. They won't leave. As soon as we get rid of one, three others materialize. They come up the back, private staff elevators. They talk Romany, no English. No one on the staff speaks Romany. I think we're going to have to bring in a platoon of police. What lovely flowers! It's not your problem."

"No. Thank God."

"Time for your noontime pills."

"Whee! Look at what we've got."

This was carried in by three nurses staggering—roses, orchids, cactuses, daisies. Astonishing. A card from every member of American Ballet Theatre, from Lucia Chase, from Oliver Smith through Mikhail Baryshnikov, whom I had never met, down to the lowest chorus girl and boy. A great big crowded card.

"Last night I called my sister in Amsterdam." (This was Maas speaking.) "I *had* to hear some Dutch."

If I could hold a book open. Or the pages of a newspaper! If my hand would hold a newspaper page! The *Times* is so big!

"When I have fears that I may cease to be before . . ."

Before—before. Not good enough. Shut it off. I've earned the right to sleep. What right?

"You know the old man who was going home with a cured thrombosis? They brought him back. He's very sick."

If I could have my hand for an hour a day! Or my

eyes. I can't make them go from line to line. I can't read. Supposing this doesn't change? Watch this! Stop it! Now.

"Wake up! Wake up! I have a sedative for you."

"I brought all of my shampoo equipment." (This is Miss Quigley.) "And tomorrow I'm going to take you downstairs so you can see people coming and going in the main hall and go into the garden."

"Garden?"

"Yes. There's a place where there are trees and growing flowers."

"Out of the dirt. Growing in the earth?"

"Yes."

Oh, how is my garden in the woods? My lost, abandoned garden, roses and lilies and bluebells and black-eyed Susans and Queen Anne's lace? And the wild flowers? How are they? Choked with weeds? Eaten by the deer or the bugs? (Choked, yes. Eaten, no.) My one little spot of color and brilliant variety lost in the woods, the great, encroaching forest. How is it faring? Who is there to see after it? No one. Nobody. And all the trees around there standing in the free afternoon, in the lovely days, and I not there to watch the light changing in their heads and down their sides and on the rocks and on the grass and on the coat of whatever wild creature steals across what had once been lawn. It will be the Fourth of July next week. It is midsummer now. I should be out there. I should be tending my garden.

On Sundays I am always old. On Sundays things have

happened before but will not happen again. On Sundays the weather never does anything so soothing as rain. It is always hard and fine and people are out doing fine things; only I'm not because I'm finished. But I have to get through the day anyway and prepare for the week, which will be the same, but in the week, what with all the people, you can't tell. The senior doctors depart Friday night, leaving a token watcher and two or three medics. These visit on Saturday in a hasty manner. On Sunday no one. So even that bizarre, incomprehensible chattering of impersonal but curious magpies is missing. And the women take over in their unvarying cleanliness. I can buy a paper. I can't hold it but I can buy it. There is no one to phone. Everyone is in the country.

I can go up on one of the roofs, Maas says. That will be a change. It takes a special fortitude and discipline to get through weekends in a New York hospital. Nothing much seems to be happening in the corridors, I think because the men are away. A hospital corridor is an extremely lively and eventful place except on weekends. Then everything stops except the toilets and the death rattles.

These glorious late June days! It is very hot on the roof, with the sun straight down, no shadows, only tar and baked gravel and heated posts and wire fencing almost too hot to touch. I pull myself along the fencing hand over hand, Maas following with the chair, to the end and back. And the sun flattens me into the chair. Yet I have achieved something. The river below is brave and glittering and makes a fine show of boats, pleasure yachts and

little speedboats, all sizes, as well as the great cement
scows moving slowly in chains, and the swift, stately Cir-
cle Line boats with loaded decks and furry wakes. And
directly opposite is Roosevelt Island with its new apartment blocks and new buses and new people like dolls, all
so hopeful and cute, all so wearying. My eyes dazzle. I
long for the shaded room and bed. Never mind, I've
achieved something and there will be a large, delicious
lunch which I'll eat or not, as I choose. And sleep.

So I leave the dazzle of the rooftop and go down to the
sick factory.

And maybe in the evening TV, except that the summer
Sunday TVs are no good and likely as not my set is broken or deliberately detached. I wakened once from a nap
to find a workman standing on a chair. (TV sets are
placed high up to accommodate prone patients.) He did
not bother to explain or reply, believing, as did all out-
siders, that since I was paralyzed I was also incompe-
tent. By the time I had summoned a nurse he had disappeared, and his office was shut until Monday. He had
detached the TV for the weekend. This happened twice.
There was no use complaining because the TV concession
is a monopoly. I heard of thefts: men in green uniforms,
like the regulars, who stood on chairs, not part of the hospital staff and therefore not part of the monopoly, independent thieves. They took the TV sets away permanently.

My Mag takes care of the TV sets and all radio sets in
her hospital in Easton. Do her patients find themselves

with no TVs over the long weekends? I'll bet they don't,
not with Mag in charge.

Sunlight on the floor. Sunlight on the bed—nice patterns. Oh, hell!

Walter will come at seven. Even on Sundays.

VIII

DROPPING the shuttle, dropping the loom, snarling the thread and clenching my teeth, looking around the therapy room I suddenly said, "I think I'll go to bed. I think I won't do any more of this. I've got a stitch in my side." And so I went to my room.

And then there it was. I was right up against it. The horror had surfaced. The waiting was over.

My memories of the exact sequence of events in the next couple of weeks is confused. I could keep no notes, not being able to write a word. Secondly, I had a great reluctance to dwell on the episodes because they were so painful to me. And, thirdly, I was doped. I think, however, after talking to the doctors and nurses, that this is more or less what happened in sequence.

It began with an unremarkable twinge of pain in my lower left side, nothing excessive, hardly noticeable except that I felt morbidly depressed and heavy and I ran a fever. The doctors expected depression, but this was what they feared, this small pain, this low-grade fever; I was in mortal peril. For this, they feared, was an embolism.

"We've all had stitches in our sides," I said.

"Yes," Plum said. "Now let's continue to talk about Catherine Drinker Bowen."

I thought he would feel my sides and my belly the way any doctor would if you said you had a pain. He didn't bother to. What I had, what he was afraid I had, could not be felt. It was instant death, floating and floating, and it must not be disturbed or joggled or teased. What he wanted to say was, "Don't move. Whatever you do, don't move." But of course he didn't say that because he would have frightened me badly. He said, "Let's talk about Catherine Drinker Bowen." But as he left he said, "No more therapy."

"Not even hand therapy?"

"No therapy at all. Not even weaving. And don't get out of bed. Call us for anything. Instantly. Do you understand that? Instantly. And I don't think you should work on your book."

Gerry worried about the abatement of the body regime. The doctors took not the slightest notice. Her worry was nothing compared to theirs.

"Her body will grow into bad habits." On the other hand, the doctors argued, the first requirement for habits of any kind is a body which is alive.

Two nights later I awoke about three in the morning with another little twinge on the left side. Obeying instructions, I had the midnight nurse call the intern, and poor Dr. Meadows, red-eyed and sleepy, stumbled to my bed. I was grovellingly apologetic. If it had only been a real pain. But it was less than I often had on the tennis courts or running for a bus.

"I'll get my stuff," he said. So he got a lot of apparatus and needles.

"I'm going to take arterial blood," he explained soothingly.

"Okay," I said, not knowing what I had agreed to.

"Way below venous blood." As though that made it better. And let me tell you, it is way below, and he took it from the left arm, which had feeling. He had to hunt around a bit for the artery, but he was extremely skillful and he only hurt me for a while, but it was drastic. And then he sealed it up with adhesives and patted me and said, "Go to sleep."

And I said, "I'm so sorry—at this hour. My God, I am sorry." And he mumbled, "Glad you did. Absolutely right." And he went away with his trophy, which apparently made quite an impression on the doctors because the next day things began to happen.

Mary Green had come up to work with me on my manuscript. The room was fetidly hot. It didn't seem so to me because I lived in it in a cotton nightshirt and a single sheet and the windows were open and the curtains stirred and there were flowers. But she had come in from the melting, sweated streets, and she was used to air cooling. I had only a very little since I could not feel cold and

might take a chill. And then there was this small compost
heap of loose papers and I was fairly excited and dicta-
torial and I couldn't bear to wait. Formerly, if I wanted
to see a page, I just found it and got to work on it. But
she was very slow, very methodical and, of course, she
wasn't me. She was somebody else, although highly
knowledgeable. In the middle of all this, nurses appeared
and said, "We've got to take an X ray." And I said something fairly obscene. And I said to Mary, "This doesn't
take long. Wait for me." She started tidying up the
flowers.

Down I went in my wheelchair and waited around for
the regulation forty to forty-five minutes with other dis-
membered subjects of the hospital. Finally I was let into
the cluttered room where all the big machinery stood and
laid on a board and told to keep my head sideways for an
hour or two. That is not an exaggeration. This X ray takes
approximately two hours. And it is not painful in any
way, just very tedious. Tick, tick, tick, tick, tick, the big
cameras swing back and forth. And you lie there ten minutes, fifteen, eighteen minutes. Well, then it begins to get
sort of strenuous because you have to keep still. Twenty-
four minutes, thirty, thirty-five, and after about forty minutes the cameras stop and somebody comes in and read-
justs the axis of the head and neck and you do some more.
I mean forty minutes more at another angle. And it is,
yes, it is about two hours. And I went back up to my
room rather tired and naturally looking forward to lunch
(it was now half past three or four), which I hoped would

be edible and which I knew was designed to be and normally would have been. (Mary had gone home, leaving a note.) And there I was, sitting and licking my chops and feeling rather contented for a job well done, when suddenly the door opened and in came the stretcher and three nurses. "Are you ready?" they said. I looked at them in simple amazement. "We've come to take you for the major X ray."

"Get me a doctor," I said. "A doctor or an intern. You don't put a finger on me until someone in authority explains to me what all this is about." And so they got my charming, kindly Dr. Meadows, who was summoned from his other duties and told to come to the irascible Prude in 910. And I looked at him in stormy protest, my teeth clenched.

"Explain," I said. So he did, lucidly and very patiently, also plainly. They were going to put iodine into my veins for photographs, so that they could have a good picture of what was going on in my venous system and would know where the clots were. That, of course, made sense, and I quieted down. And then I said to him, "Would you please do me a favor before you leave?"

He was already half out of the door and he turned back and said, "Of course I will. With pleasure. What?"

And I said, "Will you hold my hand?"

His professional manner slipped and he very gently took my left, or feeling, hand and held it. And I couldn't explain to him why I had to have his hand, but I had to

have it and he knew that and after about three minutes
he said, "Are you alright?"

And I said, "I'm alright. My husband must be told."

And he said, "Oh, yes. He has been."

And I then was taken out and left the regulation forty
minutes, during which Walter arrived, and I said, "Have
you been told?"

And he said, "Oh, yes. It's all been explained. I'll go
down with you." And we stood around and waited for a
long time.

Then I was pushed, Walter following, down to the
X-ray rooms and I was laid in the hall and was beginning
to wait the next regulation forty minutes, and Walter
said, "Now what?"

I said, "Nothing. You go get a cup of coffee."

And he said, "I think I need a drink."

And I said, "No drink in the hospital except up in my
room. You know where."

And he said, "I'll be right back."

And I said, "Don't hurry. You won't miss anything."
And he didn't hurry and he didn't miss anything. I was
still there, the identical activity going on about me, except that no new patients were being brought in, for I
was the last. It was now nearly six and everybody had
gone home. My nurse took me into the X-ray room and
there were two charming young men in their thirties, I
think, and they were absolutely alone. They had con-
sented to stay after hours and do this extremely difficult
operation, which was going to take at least three hours,

and do it alone, without assistance of any kind. And they began to explain to me what they were going to do and that it wouldn't hurt, but that it would be very lengthy and strange. Walter was taken into a viewing room where the doctors were assembled and I was left with the two young physicians below, and they took me and did what they had to.

First they had to make a chart on my body in black, wet crayon, numbered so that they could read back the X-rays. Any natural anatomical signs such as navels, nipples, and so forth, they simply disregarded. This map pertained to the venous system and nothing else, and the venous system is not readily visible on the outside of the skin. I think I must have looked very like a butcher chart hung up in the French meat shops to show where to cut for chops and roasts and steaks. Then they explained very civilly what more they were going to do. They intended to enter my groin and pour in enough iodine to circulate and be photographed. They didn't say how they'd get the iodine out again, but I supposed they'd thought of that. (Plum explained months later that the circulation carries it away.) This all seemed reasonable, but it did make me nervous to think about.

"It won't hurt," they said. "It won't hurt. You'll just feel heat." And then they anesthetized me—locally, of course—and got to work in the right groin, I presume. I couldn't feel, except slight tuggings. It took a long time and they were quite hot and I became very hot and there was a good deal of perspiration and the smell of anesthetic. And somehow in this process my nightgown seemed to get twisted up around my neck and then lost. I was stark on the table beneath their hands with only my black crayon markings to clothe me. About an hour and a half later we tried the first one. "Now, here goes," they said. "You won't feel anything but heat."

I suppose it was heat I felt. It was odd. It was intense. Well, call it heat. I don't know what else to call it. But it was unpleasant, it was . . . No, they were quite right, it wasn't painful. Then they had to do another and another. And the whole process took about three hours. They'd given up their dinner to do this. And at the end they said, "Well. Now the negatives will have all gone to be developed and we'll know in a matter of minutes."

And I said, "Gentlemen, I don't want to be finicky, but I entered with a nightgown."

"Whatever could have happened to it?" they asked, looking around, looking everywhere, under the table, under the stretcher. I think it had gotten rolled up, probably with the bloody linen, and tactfully taken away. So they threw a sheet over me.

They handled my body the way I would have managed a broken stove or toilet. I wish to interpolate here something I think is important: I was handled by those men like a piece of meat, absolutely handled and manipulated, and not once then or in any other process that transpired in the hospital did I ever feel the slightest loss of dignity, the slightest loss of personality or worth, or the slightest loss or diminution of sex. Toward me, the woman, they were respectful and kind and as helpful as they knew how to be. And this never varied in all my hospital experience. But with these two young men it was memorable because I was naked and helpless and marked up like a sacrificial calf for three hours and the three of us were alone. They were men of unblemished purity and it was, on the whole, a very nice experience spiritually.

Dr. Plum came back with my husband and some other doctors from the viewing room.

"Well, that's just fine," he said. "We discovered an enormous clot in your right leg and we'll take it away tonight."

I spoke very weakly. "I haven't had lunch."

"Oh, what good luck!" said Plum. "We can operate then all the better, although of course this is a local. This is not general." Walter was looking absolutely gray. Plum turned to him. "You can have dinner and a drink. But I imagine you'll want to be here for the operation."

"Yes," said Walter.

And I was taken out into the hall and waited two hours there. I suppose I slept.

Walter went to a friend's house and was kept alive somehow during those two hours.

They telephoned the surgeon, who was sitting down to a fine, restful meal in Alpine, New Jersey, and he had to get right up and come back and scrub up. And in two hours they took me into a green operating room and all the people in it were green. And they meant business.

"We're going to tie off the big vein in your right leg because there's a clot."

"Will there be any aftereffects?" I asked.

"Possibly," said a doctor. "I hope not. Some edema."
(Later I learned what that is: swelling.) And then they
got to work anesthetizing the leg. And the anesthetist
leaned over me and spoke quite socially through her
mask. "I had you before, a year ago, for another operation." Just as though we were at a cocktail party.

"Did you now?" I replied graciously. "How nice to
meet again." I'd never seen her mouth.

"And I'm so glad to see *you*. Indeed I'm . . ."

"I'm fainting," I interrupted rudely. She got me oxygen
and the doctors pulled and tugged as long as they had to
—an hour, I suppose; I don't know how long. And finally
it was finished. And then the surgeon said, "Now you will
go to intensive care." And I was whisked on a stretcher
upstairs without being able to do more than smile at
Walter, who had waited through the whole thing, and
was put into that strange, still, submarine place that was
like a womb.

"Where is my signal light? I must have my light," I
said, "so I can summon a nurse."

"You will have a nurse here every two minutes all night
long."

"I need a blanket," I said. "I'm chilly."

"You won't need a blanket and this is the atmosphere.
You'll adjust to it in just a few seconds. It will never
change."

What a day this had been! What a long, long day, be-ginning with literary exercises with Mary Green and now this peculiar place. Oh, so strange and unfamiliar! This strange, unborn light, with everybody walking in rubber soles and talking in whispers and lights coming and lights going and people on the brink of death all around, half-alive, half-dead, and not a breath, not a pulse but was known immediately and registered and coped with. Or not coped with. But known. How many people died that night right beside me? I was not told, nor did I hear. In the morning I found I had survived and ate an absolutely antiseptic breakfast. I was deemed ready to go home to my room and was wheeled by a sweet, pretty nurse from this elite brigade. And when she got me into the room she actually said, "Well, good-bye and good luck. It's been nice having you."

And I said, "Those are the first really feeling words that I've heard from a regular nurse, but I suppose you're special." And she winked at me.

I was very tired, very tired, and they had told me not to move my leg and not to wiggle around. Out of the question. I was tired.

Plum comments on these events:

Agnes de Mille's account describes accurately the symp-toms of pulmonary embolism, a dreaded complication of illness and bed rest. When a human being takes to bed with sickness, injury or surgery, his or her body mobilizes a number of innate defenses. One of these defenses acts to protect us against potential blood loss by enhancing the blood's clotting capacity. As can be true with other physiologic safeguards, the response sometimes can exceed the need, so that clots form spontaneously in certain relatively stagnant venous pools. Such clots (thromboses) are especially prone to collect in the deeper veins of the lower legs, where their formation characteristically escapes detection by patient or doctor. Undoubtedly, in many patients such thromboses accumulate and later dissolve spontaneously without producing ill effects. Often, however, they slowly enlarge with looser and looser ends, until fragments break off, iceberglike, into smaller or larger pieces which drift in the venous current to the heart and thence the lungs. Small pulmonary emboli often produce no symptoms and go clinically unnoticed. Larger ones create a serious threat and may cause chest pain, shortness of breath or even death.

Agnes de Mille's body, partially stilled these several weeks, created notoriously ideal circumstances for the development of deep venous thrombosis. We had worried about this from the start, but the risk of re-initiating bleeding in her head made it appear too dangerous to give her anticoagulant medicines, as the drugs that prevent clotting are called. So we settled on having the nurses and therapists passively move and stretch her limbs several times each day, beginning gently within the first day after the onset of her stroke. It was now obvious that these halfway measures hadn't done the hoped-for job.

Miss de Mille doesn't remember it now, but the first

danger sign had turned up about two weeks before the more dramatic episode struck, as she described it in the preceding section. One afternoon after physical therapy she complained of a vague ache in the right side of her chest, perhaps made worse by taking deep breaths or moving the right arm. We closely examined her legs and chest and took blood tests and chest X rays. None of these showed any new abnormality. Some tenderness in the chest wall suggested that she might have had no more than a therapy-induced muscle strain. But we watched as she says, like hawks. And despite her undeniable social charms, that was the major reason for the many close visits and the indirect, hopefully unfrightening, conversations. Was there a hidden killer? And if it attacked again, would we have time to disarm it? Again the decision involved high stakes: Does one subject a dangerously debilitated older woman to painfully weakening diagnostic procedures based on a brief and possibly benign symptom, or do the odds say wait—and risk a potentially fatal clot? We waited.

The second attack dictated no safe alternative other than to act vigorously and immediately. Laboratory studies indicated a telltale impairment of oxygenation of the blood by the lungs and X rays of the chest taken after the injection of radioisotopes showed a density in the left lung unmistakably produced by a clot. Nothing about the lung shadow, of course, said where the clot arose, although the veins of the paralyzed leg were the obvious main contender. But one could not be sure or perform an appropriate surgical attack at this "mother" clot without more direct evidence. Indeed, the veins of the other leg or even those draining the lower trunk provided almost equal chances of being involved either alone or together.

The events that Miss de Mille describes followed during the late afternoon and evening of the day when that second chest pain hit. By late that afternoon she was in the X-ray department, where radiologists injected dye at two points into her leg to outline the circulation of blood in the veins in the lower extremities, the trunk and the lungs. Sure enough, a large clot filled the remote veins in the right leg. In the lungs the presence of several blocked vessels in regions beyond the already recognized area on the left re-emphasized how often multiple emboli can occur without producing either obvious symptoms or visible shadows on the X ray. That night vascular surgeons tied off the main vein draining the right leg. Henceforth blood would find its way from that leg toward the heart by travelling through more devious and much less dangerous channels.

With the operation successfully finished, we breathed more easily, but the problem had not completely passed.

They promised they'd solved this problem. They were wrong.

The terrible weakness continued, the mounting fatigue, the hopeless fear. I was out of my depth. I knew it. On the outside there was no sign of any kind. There was no clue at all as to what was wrong with me. But the doctors knew with the first X ray that there were several emboli lodged in my chest. Walter was shown a photograph of them, dark masses, the mark of death. They had not excised the danger.

My wanderings on the rooftop and other journeys were curtailed by the tubes. Dr. Plum had thought to prevent blood clotting by blood thinning, so my veins were attached to bottles of liquid. That only changed my life inasmuch as it reduced it.

I have said repeatedly that nothing ever happened on the weekends, except that it seemed always that on the weekends the big accidents occurred.

The weekend after my iodine arteriogram X ray, with the clot removed from my leg, Dr. Plum came in on Friday afternoon and said, "Don't you dare do anything while I'm gone this weekend. Mind now." And he patted my cheek and went off placidly to his vegetable garden in Long Island.

On this Friday, another lesser chest pain hit, producing a new small shadow in the lung. Most likely a postoperative, hopefully smaller, clot had formed at the point where the ligation had been placed around the femoral (large leg) vein. Further surgery higher up would be possible, but this represented a major undertaking, perhaps more than Miss de Mille's body could withstand. Considering the risk of brain bleeding now at a low ebb and less of a threat than that of more pulmonary emboli, we reluctantly started anticoagulant drugs. But she's right. The decision required that we attend to things more important than a vegetable garden in the country.

But I learned later that, in fact, he did not go off to his vegetable garden; in fact, he stayed in New York.

He knew that the entire floor staff was due to change on July 1, and he did not want doctors unfamiliar with my case left alone with the responsibility. He gave up his Fourth of July weekend and remained in the hospital a good part of the time, came in frequently to see me while I slept, and watched the charts all night long. That's how dangerous my situation was. All along he did not make himself visible to me or come to me because he did not wish to terrify me, and this is where his great art became manifest.

Dr. Plum had asked me after the operation to tell him how I felt; he wanted to know my version. He pretended the blood clot in my leg had been expected and was casual. (In fact, it was expected alright, but feared; it was not casual. The doctors were watching me hawk-eyed.)

Plum said later he had wanted to say that week, "Don't move. Don't move an arm. Don't move a leg. Don't move a hand. Don't breathe suddenly." But he couldn't say this without causing me to die of terror. So instead he said, "Move as little as is comfortable." If I were joggled, if I were pushed brusquely, if I toppled, the whole blood balance might be destroyed and the deadly enemies, more emboli, dislodged and freed to go straight to my heart, which is where all blood flows, returning to be renewed, including the blood with the clots. This was destined to go to the heart also. Two weeks passed this way.

Walter went off for the July 18 weekend for the first time since May 15. He took Mary and Jonathan with him. They had nothing special in mind. They just wanted to sit in the woods and breathe quietly.

It began late Friday afternoon. My sister woke me on the phone. She was in New York at the Harkness Pavilion again, having more chemotherapy. I'd been in the hospital so long that she had been up to New York twice for monthly treatments. This was her second time at the Harkness. She rang me about five o'clock to talk. Before the stroke I had always wakened instantly, fully alert. Indeed, I could have jumped from the bed to the podium and made a public speech. But after the stroke I was slow to wake, muddled, vacant. My sister went on affably, full of anecdote, full of comment, asking questions, answering them, explaining before I had time to reply, laughing, laughing a great deal without realizing that I had not joined in. She was mortally ill and she was spending herself to entertain me this weary afternoon. But what made me panic was not that I couldn't get a word in (that was usual with Margaret) but that I couldn't get a word out at all. I couldn't speak. I found this out in three syllables. I finally managed "doctors" or something like that. She plunged into a good-bye, loving and wordy. I grunted and hung up and flashed for Quigley. I tried to say, "It's difficult to speak." Gobbledygook.

Quigley fled, returning with young Dr. Meadows. He took one look and went into action like a fireman, pulling out all the needles and taking my blood pressure, giving me pills to counteract what they had steadily dripped into my veins, and taking my blood pressure again and yet again. And leaving and coming back with reinforcements.

Again they asked me questions. What day of the week was it? I couldn't remember. What were the questions? The week? The year of my birth? The name of the doctor? His wristwatch? I was frightened. I had missed the rung of the ladder. I couldn't hold on. It was like falling asleep, falling, falling away. But I wasn't falling asleep. I was mixed up. My name . . . Oh, please, never again. Pain, maybe, even pain, but ME.

"Quiet," said Quigley. "It will be alright." She never left my side for an instant.

In fifty minutes I could say an English sentence.

"It's coming back," said Quigley, bathing my forehead. "You're going to be alright."

"I'm frightened."

"These episodes are very common. They're not serious. Try to rest."

A half hour later I said, without slurring, "I lost my mind."

We use that phrase—how often? But, you see, I had done just exactly that, and the terrifying aspect was that I knew every second just how far I was out of control. Who was ME without memory?

Dr. Meadows came in the next morning and sat down quietly.

"You must not be scared by this. It's very usual. It happens in these cases. It happens with this medicine, but it's brief and it will become less and less frequent. It is quite ordinary. You have got to expect it." Well, that cheered me up a lot. I called Merriewold and by great good luck got Jonathan on the phone.

"When you answer, don't show any alarm of any sort."

"Alright," he said.

"Something happened to me yesterday and it would be a comfort to me if I knew you were coming home tonight. Don't stay up there in the woods. I mustn't be alone."

"Alright," he said. "We'll be right back."

And so they were, the poor things, having just got there. But, you see, I was so terribly frightened.

On Monday evening Dr. Plum came in and sat down for his usual chat.

"What happened?" he said. "Tell me exactly and tell me everything."

So I told him and I added, "It's nothing, of course. Dr. Meadows said it happens very frequently and is quite ordinary and not to be wondered at or to be worried about."

"Hmm," said Plum.

"Does it worry you?"

"Hmm," said Plum. "We've got to find out what it is

that's throwing emboli into your system. We've simply got to find out."

"How can you do that?" I said.

"Well, we have ways." And then he began to talk about writing and literature and Elizabethan slang and various matters that interested both of us and about which he was enchanting.

They had ways indeed, and I was to learn them. Every one of them.

Dr. Plum comments at this point:

> When the new neurological symptoms developed, our immediate worry was that under the influence of the anticoagulants, she had bled into her brain again. The speech loss, although brief, reduplicated that which accompanied the first stroke, pointing to new trouble in the same part of the brain and possibly implying a weakness of the vessels in that area.

First they did another CAT scan to tell if it was a new hemorrhage. It wasn't and Plum came in and said, "Agnes, this is going to be more difficult. I think you have a clot in one of the arteries going to your brain. But thinking isn't enough. We have to know. If there is such a clot, the parent clot, it could cause more strokes. On the other hand, and even more important, the clot might be at a place where the surgeons can remove it. And *that* approach might protect you against any more brain damage. But we must first do a test, called an arteriogram, to be exactly sure where the clot lies. The test will be uncomfortable and it can sometimes be hazardous. We'll have our most skilled people at every point along the line. And we'll do the best we know how. But there is some risk. Do you want us to go ahead?"

What the hell! One more test—dangerous, smangerous—I didn't give it a thought. I wanted them to get on with the business and finish. This lolling around and waiting while I got weaker and weaker was no good.

Plum had always been careful not to frighten me, but he had to ask me this question by law. He had to get my permission, not Walter's. Mine, while I was conscious.

Dr. Plum goes on:

The technique of cerebral angiography, as the radiographic outlining of the arterial tree of the brain is called, was invented over fifty years ago. At the time it represented a leap forward in diagnostic methods almost as great as Hounsfield's later discovery of CAT scanning. Egas Moniz, a Portuguese neurologist, conceived and originated a method of injecting into the brain's arteries material that casts an X-ray shadow and thereby delineated the arterial anatomy on film. Between 1927 and 1930 Moniz refined the procedure sufficiently to show its usefulness in human beings, his ingeniousness winning him a Nobel Prize in 1949.

Unfortunately, the procedure of arteriography, although greatly improved in recent years, still imposes certain dangers on the patient; these risks increase in older persons and in those with high blood pressure and vascular disease. But in Agnes de Mille's case the march of illness left little doubt that the arteries should be examined. The hazards imposed by avoiding the procedure and thereby overlooking an important treatable abnormality were too great. Furthermore, the risk can be considerably reduced by first inserting a catheter into a leg artery and then passing it forward under X-ray visualization so its tip lies at the base of the neck vessels.

Arteriography done in this manner is relatively nonhazardous, although, as with many complex procedures in medicine, difficulties on rare occasions result from inadvertent lapses in technique. Much more often, however, complications, when they occur, reflect the inherent potential problems created by doing the procedure on very ill patients. Passage of the catheter up the aorta or into a carotid artery can break a piece of arteriosclerotic debris away from the inner vessel wall, whence it may be carried by the arterial flow to produce an embolus in a remote organ. Similarly, tiny unsuspected clots sometimes form on the tip of the catheter to form emboli. On rare occasions the catheter can tear the smooth inner intimal surface of an artery, creating a risk of plugging it. Happily, none of these complications accompanied Agnes de Mille's examination.

IX

EVERY human body is different and the doctors proceeded without any recipe for mine. Like country cooks trying a little more of this, more mustard, there were clots; a little less of that, less pepper, a hemorrhage, only—and this is important—it was I who did the tasting and I who had to do the digesting.

They had ways.

As I was going down for the big test, being wheeled away by the orderlies, a floor nurse, faithful and good, ran to me and leaned over me.

"Good luck" she whispered and patted my cheek. The floor nurse did that! And then I knew I was going to face something very, very difficult.

It was an empty room except for the tray on which I was to go and the monster machine, enormous, hooded, full of lights.

"This is your doctor," someone said. "This is your surgeon, Dr. Potts."

"Good morning."

"Ah, you're English," I said affably.

"No. New Zealand."

"Oh, that's nice. A beautiful country."

He had turned his back and was huddled over mechanics. He had no time for scenery. His assistant was introduced. I gathered it was a female, but as to age or kind I couldn't guess. Masked. The doctor adjusted his mask. Another attendant took charge of the upper half.

"I am here to help you and explain."

"That's nice."

"There will be no pain. None whatever."

"That's nice."

"Now we are giving you the anesthetic." They had uncovered my lower regions.

"We'll use the right femoral artery. Ah! What is this?"

"Somebody has been there before," I said. I was still black and purple. I think somebody said, "Whew!" But I might have been wrong.

"Well, then we'll use the left. Shave this."

So they shaved another portion of me. They only shaved what they had to work with. They were very delicate about that. So there were sections of flesh left matted with hair, I suppose. I must have looked like the head of a Zulu. Well, they got that done. And then they said, "Now this is the needle. You will feel a prick." And I did, because that was the side of me that still felt things. And they said, "Now we're going deeper and deeper with the anesthetic." And, of course, I felt nothing. And they went deeper and deeper and they waited very patiently for the anesthetic to take effect and then they went deeper and deeper.

"Now," they said, "she's ready."

"Ah," said the surgeon, moving in. And my attendant, who seemed like a secretary—I remember her with a sweater and skirt and a secretarial pad (but, of course, that is complete nonsense. She was dressed like a nurse, without a cap, but I do think she had a sweater)—said, "There will be no pain. Absolutely none."

"That's good," I said.

"I will tell you everything that's going to happen. I will explain everything."

"Thank you."

And then after a while she said, "Now they are going to insert the tube." And I began feeling pulling and tugging, but nothing more. I felt the pulling and tugging because the other nerves of my body were still alive.

"I feel nothing," I said.

"You can't feel. They're into the artery," she said. "Arteries don't feel."

"Is that so? How interesting! No arteries feel?"

Reader, I tell you this because I think it is indeed interesting. Once you get inside an artery you feel nothing. Of course you have to get *inside* first and there's a great deal of matter outside that feels all the way. But once you're inside, Nirvana!

And then she said (now this, you know, was an hour later), "They are now getting the tube into place. That won't take long." That didn't take very long, roughly twelve minutes, inch by inch by inch. I didn't know how long the tube was. It was actually about twenty-five inches long. And there was a long piece of it hanging out for safety's sake, I was told, so they could pull it out again without losing it. The mind boggles—and so would the bloodstream, no doubt, without this safety tab, because naturally it would get slippery and it would be a damn nuisance if it got lost inside my arteries. Well, they got that settled in finally. We'd been at it for about an hour and forty minutes, patiently, patiently, quietly, the surgeon and his assistants muttering down at their end, a towel screening me from vision and sound. I didn't really want to see what they were doing. And my translator up at my end told me every step of the way. And I kept saying, "You don't need to explain. I really don't want to know. Just tell me if there's going to be pain or if there's going to be trouble."

"No pain. Absolutely no pain."

"Well, now we're ready," they said, and the surgeon came up to my end. And into the room, if you please, came Dr. Fred Plum in a business suit, very spruce, and he said, "I'm watching this because it's so interesting and so important."

"How kind of you!"

"Well," they said, "now we're going to pour in iodine and it will go all through your arteries and up past your lungs and heart and that is the reason for the operation. And as it passes your lungs and heart we photograph it and we will have to leave the room because it's X ray."

"Now," said the assistant at my end, "no pain, no pain but great heat. You will feel great heat and you mustn't be surprised. Don't move. Don't move anything, not your head, not your neck, not your shoulders. Keep perfectly still for the camera."

"I'll try," I said. "Trust me."

"Certainly," she said. And with that somebody—I think a man—took a two-inch-wide surgical tape and placed it across my face and head, across the upper lip, taped it flat to the table and then took a two-inch-wide surgical tape and taped it across my chin. I couldn't move a lip or a nostril. You can't scream with your mouth gagged. Anybody knows that.

What I actually thought about at the moment with astonished wonder yet overwhelming clarity was what made the doctors ever think of doing this. How did they find they could? What poor wretch was first experimented on? What poor, poor animals came first? The first time they probably poured something in that was not harmless and that made the patient feel a great deal more than just heat.

"Now, here goes" said the surgeon and, I guess, poured in iodine. I could, of course, feel nothing. And then they ran for it, literally scrambling, and slammed the door shut and were behind glass, safe, watching the death chamber, leaving me alone.

And the medicine mounted in my bloodstream at the rate of my blood flow. And it's pretty fast, faster than I had thought; that much I could feel. One, two, three, four . . . Gone! The roof lifted. The lid was off. There was no top.

Help! Help! My teeth went. The eyeballs held by a string. Air! Help! No top. No head.

They were coming back into the room. Somebody yanked off the adhesive.

"Well, that's fine. That's absolutely fine."

I was panting.

In came Dr. Plum and took my hand, the one I could feel with, and said, "You're just marvelous. You photograph like a Hollywood star. Nobody has ever photographed better."

"Oh, good girl," said the assistant. "Good girl! You didn't move."

"I couldn't. You know I couldn't. I tried. I couldn't. You fixed it so I couldn't."

"There, there now. That's marvelous," said the surgeon. "Simply wonderful."

"Now," said the assistant, "now, you see, we only have to do it two more times."

When they came in the third time, just a little bit jaded, and I lay there panting, with the adhesive tape strewn about the pillow beside me, I said, "You know, you could become addicted to this. There really is quite a bang in it." Nobody listened. Nobody laughed. The surgeon was doing something or other and I said, "Doctor, may I ask one question? I haven't asked any questions." He nodded. "Since you were into me so far, why is there no blood?"

"Oh," he said, "we're careful."

Well, that's very neat and tidy, I thought. And then they were wheeling me out of the room with the assistant surgeon helping me. And she turned out to be a very young and very attractive Canadian girl, I guess about twenty-eight years old, in a canary yellow jumper. And, as I looked out of the corner of my eye, there was a lot of blood, but they were bundling the sheets up into a huddle and taking it all away.

They were finished with me.

She took me to another room and said, "I have to take out the tube."

"Oh, do," I said. "Pray do." And I lay there on the pallet and in came my physical therapist, Gerry Donato, and I said, "What are you doing here?" And she said, "I'm interested." Well, she really had no business to attend to there, but she had permission and she sat there patting me on the side on which I couldn't feel and she and the assistant surgeon had an interesting conversation about this and that. And I said, "Tell me, do you ever go higher?"

"Oh my, yes," the young surgeon said. "Goodness, this is nothing. We have tubes that go into the heart and even into the brain, and it was just such a tube that killed . . ." I thought she said Rod Steiger.

"Oh, no!" I said. "How terrible! I knew him."

"Well, he died three days ago of just such an operation."

I must say that I was at a loss for comment. It turned out later it was not Rod Steiger at all, but Rod something or other.

And then I looked down—they were not being so careful now—and there was the tube, slimy, not bloody, just slimy, and it was about three and a half feet long, of good, stout rubber.

"You had *that* in me?" I said.

"Yes," she said, hiding it rather shamefacedly, as though it were a public nuisance that had been committed on the rug.

In came my nurse, my own, true, beloved Maas.

"You've got to go rest," she said. "This is very tiring."

"Is it, now!" I said.

The next day I turned black. I'm not speaking metaphorically. I am speaking exactly. The entire groin and thigh went black and plum-colored and dark purple. In two weeks there were streaks of poison green through it and in three and a half weeks it had faded to a lovely soft saffron. I never saw human flesh so misused in all my life. But they were quite used to it up there and they expected it.

So the arteries feel nothing, do they? Well, well! Another human organ that feels nothing is the brain. There it sits, complacently impervious, and knows no pain, but

brush it with a piece of gauze and the individual is paralyzed. Frown at it and he is speechless. You'd better be
careful about the brain alright! Try keeping oxygen from
it; six minutes and you have idiocy; ten minutes and there
is permanent coma, as with Karen Anne Quinlan, the
New Jersey comatose marvel.

The next evening Dr. Plum came in to me. "We found
it. We found the seat of your troubles."

"Where?" I said.

"In the carotid artery." (That's in the neck.) "We've
seen in the X ray what we think it is; we think it's the
'mother clot,' so to speak, the big clot that is throwing off
the emboli. We've got to remove this."

He explained briefly that they were going to slit my
throat. I opened my eyes. "But the doctor to do this, Dr.
Patterson, is not here in New York, so we must wait a
week. We don't want to wait, but we think we will. He is
the Tiffany, the Heifetz of surgeons for this operation.
He's the absolute best, and he's worth waiting for, because we need his opinion as well as his skill. We have the
medicine to protect you while waiting. It's a rather tricky
operation."

"How tricky?"

"Oh, well. He can do it easily." (Slitting the throat and
putting in a plastic pipe? Pooh!) "But I want *him* to do
it.

"We're going to put you back on heparin, the blood
thinner."

Plum continues:

Miss de Mille had had high blood pressure for a long while, and her electrocardiogram showed evidence of past heart damage. More serious, her whole physical and spiritual being had been badly assaulted by a near-fatal brain injury. During recent weeks, pulmonary embolism and surgery on the leg had wrung out of her much of her remaining resistance. Added to all of this, Miss de Mille had been undergoing an exhausting physical exercise program aimed at counteracting her paralysis and restoring her mobility. The excellent judgment of the surgeon, Russel Patterson, Jr., and my long experience of working together with him as a medical-surgical team outweighed, in my mind, the possible advantages of operating immediately after the arteriogram gave us the diagnosis. I wanted her to have Russel Patterson's opinion and the potential benefit of his dexterity before she took that big step.

The events surrounding the surgery are such that older patients and those with serious heart or vascular disease pose a greater than normal risk. Such individuals carry perhaps one chance in twenty of developing a serious stroke or even dying after the operation. Because of these factors, Agnes de Mille's situation was delicate enough to deserve our getting several additional opinions from both physicians and the neurosurgeon before deciding to proceed. All the consultants agreed that the threat of leaving nature alone was greater than the combined risks of anesthesia, surgery and the postoperative period.

But we had to wait a week and the doctors and, of course, Walter held their breaths.

These were the nights when I faced it, the fact; I was for it; I was going to die. I thought, this is where we close the parenthesis, b. 1910–d. 1975, and, ready or not, admired or not, with or without prayer, this was when. And it didn't matter how bright I was, or how witty or skillful, this was when; it happened this way, little by little strength went out, energy drained like water in the sand, each day I couldn't do more; and then I wasn't. I was not a believer, I was a wonderer. One day I would stop wondering. This is the fact.

When I realized that I was going to die, my first reaction was not so much terror but affront. That this could happen to me now, before I was ready, before I'd done the big works I intended to do and was surely worthy of; that this could happen unexpectedly and immediately to me, who had to be present, of necessity, in order to notice, in order to keep track, because, obviously, if I were not present I could not keep track, and who, then, would? I had never thought consciously of myself as important, but of course, in common with all other humans, I felt that I was the pivot, the point of view, of the world. And to think of life continuing in its daily way without me there (the me who remembered, the me who noticed—but not for long now) was very nearly incomprehensible. At bad times in the past I had been able to imagine wishing to snuff out, wishing for surcease, but now I did not wish for anything of the sort. And now I was faced with just that. And the second reaction was anger at the impudence of fate, that it was to happen now, just draining away without a pain, without a noise, without any possible climax. Once, a long time ago, I had nearly drowned, swept out to sea in a riptide. I remember my extreme surprise at finding that although I swam with all my might, I made no progress against the current but simply drifted farther and farther away. Finally two young, beautiful men rescued me, each grabbing an arm and shouting, "Throw up your legs and let us pull!" And it took all their strength to do it.

But in this crisis there were no young, beautiful men. And I was drifting farther and farther from shore. Quietly but very definitely, each day I was weaker. "You're going to die," I said to myself. "This really is it and you had better say something definitive, something that will sum up your life."

The necessity to pronounce harassed me because, quite frankly, I could think of nothing to say. And I fretted through the long hours until it occurred to me, in the middle of the night, that I really didn't need to say anything at all. Nobody expected it or even wanted it. Having talked all my life ceaselessly, it seemed likely that if I hadn't said what I'd meant to say by now, it wasn't from lack of trying, and that, in fact, my whole life was what I had to say; my habits of living were my statements, some terminal bon mot was not. With this relaxing idea I let myself drift back into sleep untormented.

The next day I was very much weaker, very much sicker. I couldn't understand why. I couldn't understand anything, but I felt lost and helpless and I was scared to the marrow. That evening I said to Plum, "I'm scared to death." And it was the truth. And, truthfully, the entire medical staff was indeed extremely concerned. And I huffed and I puffed and all that happened was that I grew weaker. I was failing in every possible way, but I think Plum was fond enough to be even a little frightened.

"Don't you dare give up," he said. "Keep your pecker up." (Actually I didn't know what a pecker was. It was Antony Tudor who explained it later to me and then I thought the remark cheery but inappropriate. As a matter of historical philological fact, the word derives from *pécour*, meaning with heart. In other words, the comment means "Keep your heart strong." However . . .)

Dr. McCagg said later, very much later, "You were the sickest patient I ever had." And as I preened rather and looked smug, even boastful, she continued, "The sickest that lived."

But I knew that it was hair-trigger. And the doctors huddled in the hall and Plum kept hoping that the emboli wouldn't move and that he could get me through another twelve hours because, in all honesty, no one ever knew when he came back in the morning what word would greet him. He knew I surely should not remain lucky and skirt this mortal danger that threatened me every time my heart beat. He and two or three of the others lived in constant apprehension of the expected phone call. And so did my poor Walter, who had ben alerted to the exact peril and who had been shown a photograph of my chest with the visible threats lodged very near my heart.

"Try not to move around much," they said without explaining why. And the doctors steadfastly strove, one way and another, to keep me alive with treatments, devices I have somewhat forgotten or confused. And every day and every night Plum kept watch.

I saw only Walter and I saw him only for the briefest time. Poor darling. He wandered New York alone, taking asylum with friends. He was desperate. He couldn't believe what was happening.

It was at this point that he called Margaret and said, "She's going. I can't save her. I can't stop her. What shall I do?" And he was in total despair.

And Margaret said, "Walter, I'm flat on my back with tubes stuck in me and I can do nothing." And those two poor souls said what they could to one another, and I am sure Margaret said helpful things because she was strong.

He went to Mary Green and walked the streets with her, and she followed along without talking because there was nothing whatever she could say. I did not know this until very much later, and he does not recall the full agony. Mary and Margaret did.

These were the long nights. These were the small hours when the world held its breath, waiting, waiting, and these were the nights when my wonderful nurse, Miss

Jackson, sat with me, talking wisely and sweetly about her experiences.

Miss Jackson, my lovely, elderly American night nurse (oh, what a comfort these expert, elderly, quiet women were, with their starched caps and their pristine uniforms and their quiet, skillful hands and quiet, sympathetic voices) chosen very specially by the head nurse for a bad situation. She took the ghastly session, midnight to morning, particularly fearful before and after operations.

She had lived with dying soldiers. She'd been around the world and she'd seen more people die (and be born, presumably) than there are hours in the year. She talked about the men who had faced just precisely what I was facing, but with less chance and less care. And after she'd spoken a little bit, she always went and made me a lovely hot cup of tea in the real English style, and we had that together, even at four o'clock in the morning, so that I could sleep.

"There was a boy in Guam," said my nurse, "whose leg had been blown off. Drollest boy I ever met . . ."

And then one sundown in came Dr. Patterson, young, well, I suppose in his late forties, dark, Scotch, marvelous looking. And he said, "How do you do. How do you feel?"

And I cut right through the polite chatter and came to the point. "Doctor," I said, "they've put considerable pressure on you to do this delicate operation."

And he smiled. "Nobody puts pressure on me. This decision is between you and me entirely."

And I said something polite to the effect, "Don't be an ass." I did clearly say, "How can I possibly voice an opinion? I don't know anything."

And he said, "Well, you have a choice, you know. It's your neck. You can choose not to submit to the operation and avoid all the discomfort of the operation, which is considerable though not excessive. And there is always a certain danger with the knife. (For me, with my clotting record, it was a sixty-forty chance, but I did not know this.) You know that. But it's not a bad risk. Or you can take your chances with never having another episode. But you will run the risk of having another stroke. And in that case I think you might never speak again."

And I said, "That's quite a choice. When do you think you could do the operation?"

And he said, "Tomorrow morning at eight."

And I said, "But I'm not prepared."

And he said, "They're outside in the hall." And he opened the door and in came his troop and prepared me for an operation at eight. The troop was so overcome with giggles at a private joke that they could hardly do the job, and they certainly couldn't answer my questions, until I called back the one female among them and said, "Doctor, in the name of pity, what is going to happen to me tomorrow morning?" She told me exactly, and it was drastic.

"How does one survive?" I said.

"Oh, you do," she said very gently and patted me and went off to rejoin the gigglers.

That night was difficult. But there was my lovely elderly American, Miss Jackson. She could make me no tea because they wouldn't let me have any liquid after eleven o'clock, not one drop. But she sat beside me and she talked very quietly, very sweetly. And she held onto the rope and I held onto my end and we were hanging on for my life. And, of course, she knew it. And the hours went by and I thought, "This is it." And I thought, "But I've known this since I was old enough to know anything. There would be a time when I would face it. And this is it." And I thought, "But everybody faces this. Every single globule on the earth that ever achieves life faces this. And every single person resists it. And then it happens. And the substance goes on. And it's a big, big experience, but the substance goes on. It will happen at eight o'clock tomorrow morning. Up until the lights go out it will be interesting."

And I said to her, "If I could have my lips moistened . . ."

And she said, "Certainly. But you cannot drink anything." And she said, "Try to rest." She said, "I will be with you until six."

It was at this moment, this black moment, the nadir of my life, that Kate Medina, my editor at Doubleday, sent word to me that they would indeed publish the book and would be waiting for the manuscript. I looked at the pile of disreputable papers across the room, under their surgical towel, on their surgical table, but I had the promise,

and this promise went with me the next day into the operating room.

At six they all came in and started with needles and
things. And it *was* interesting. At eight I went down to
the operating theater and they were all in green again.
And it was for real. This was no local. And they said,
"Now we're giving you a shot in the arm and you won't
know anything." And then they came in with all their
shaving apparatus and cut off my head hair, a great portion of it, and I didn't know what happened after that.

Four hours later I woke up, hooded with bandages, just
a funnel to achieve life with, just my eyes, which were
swollen, and my mouth, which was crusted with blood,
and the terrible pain in my mouth and throat, and the rest
of me hooded like an undersea swimmer about 1903 in
the great depth masks. And I croaked, "Can I have my
mouth moistened?" So they moistened my lips, but they
didn't let me drink. And I choked and choked and I struggled for breath and the slime went down my throat and
choked me. And I said, "Will you raise my head?"

And they said, "No."

And then I said, "Please raise my head." Nobody answered. And then I said, "Please help me." Nobody answered. This went on for three and a half to four hours.
And I could not make anyone listen to me. Occasionally
someone came over and peered and said nothing at all
and went away.

Upstairs in my room, or downstairs, my husband
walked the floor and smoked and walked the floor. I was

supposed to be back in my room by twelve at the latest, he was told. The operation had been at eight-thirty. By three-thirty he called the surgeon, Dr. Patterson, and said, "For God's sake, where's my wife?"

And the surgeon said, "Mrs. Prude? Oh my God!" And then there was a pause and he said, "She'll be right with you." (You can fill in the rest of that. Plainly, everyone had forgotten about me.)

And when I came into the room croaking and muttering, Walter said later that I looked perfectly monstrous, taped and black with blood, and the mouth pulled all out of shape by the tubes, and the clamps and bandages out six inches from my head. He held my hand, the good one, and he kissed something, whatever was visible, and they washed my face and they gave me a drink. And then the pain began and the awful discomfort. And Walter left because he couldn't stand it and he couldn't help.

Inside the mummy of bandages I just fought to endure. Dr. Plum says:

> Dr. Patterson removed uneventfully from the inside of the partially obstructed carotid artery a one-and-one-half-inch-long arteriosclerotic crust covered with loose and dangerous surface material. Blood flowed freely again through the now fully open channel.
>
> A major factor that has improved the safety and success of delicate neurosurgical and vascular procedures, such as endarterectomy, has been the development of effective anesthetic methods. The anesthesiologist works

mainly in the semiremote world of the operating and recovery rooms, where patients barely come to know him.
Yet his skills can make the critical difference between un-
complicated success and a stormy surgical and postoperative course. To the anesthesiologist falls the responsibility
for assuring the patient's easy and calm transition from
awareness to painless sleep, as well as supervising his
medical well-being during and immediately after surgery. Full anesthesia, which provides maximal protection
against complications, often requires that at the beginning
of the operation the anesthesiologist insert an airway tube
directly into the body's main windpipe, the trachea. Such
endotracheal tubes extend below the vocal cords, thereby
guaranteeing that the cords won't suddenly and inadvert-
ently close to obstruct the airway during the operation.
Such intubation also makes it possible to assure satisfac-
tory expansion of the lungs with life-sustaining oxygen. As
the surgeon closes the wound, the anesthesiologist light-
ens the anesthesia and gently withdraws the tube, usually
just before the patient awakens. Not surprisingly, the intubation sometimes bruises the vocal cords and temporary
hoarseness follows for the first few postoperative days. So
it was with Miss de Mille.

Postoperatively, Miss de Mille was fine, given the circumstances. She awoke almost as soon as her skin was
stitched back together and was sent promptly to the postoperative recovery room, where teams of nurses and doctors watch all postoperative cases constantly for the least
sign of trouble. There, Patterson, myself—all of us so con-

cerned with her care—tested, poked and questioned her until we were satisfied that all parts moved as well as they had before the operation and that her hoarse croaks made sense. Reassured, we left and she drifted into the period of amnesic postanesthetic bliss which often later escapes the memory.

It certainly escaped mine.

My wonderful American nurse had been preempted by a previous engagement and could not be with me, although she did sneak down the hall to visit me for a few minutes at a time.

But I had been canny enough to order a private nurse, although Dr. Patterson had said, "No need, of course, no need. It's an easy operation. You'd be up and walking around—if you could walk—by the next day." Well, I gagged and choked and stifled inside the cocoon. And after they laid me down that night, I gagged and choked and then I said, "I've got a pain in my chest. An embolism is back." And they sent for the intern and darling Dr. Meadows came in and I said, "The pain is back. I've got an embolism."

And he said, "Don't be a fool. You haven't. We took it away."

And I said, "Haven't I?"

And he said, "No, you haven't. You're perfectly safe."

And I said, "Can I count on that?"

And he said, "yes" and patted me flat.

And I said, "Well, one thing (mind you, I was croaking, not speaking), one thing is certain. I'm going to throw up." And he put his arms around me and held me and I threw up all over him and all over me.

And he said, "Go ahead, do some more." So I did some more. And the mummy threw up and threw up and was empty. And he wiped himself clean, I guess, and changed his tunic and they cleaned me up and I went back to the agony for the rest of the night. I couldn't breathe except sitting straight up, and my nurse, who was a Filipino, began to be very impatient with the fact that she couldn't sit down for two minutes because of my choking and spewing, and she had to clean me up constantly. She propped me up and I finally found I could breathe for two and a half minutes sitting straight up, but it went on and on and by morning I was exhausted. We both were. And the doctors came in and I said, "I'm tired. I'm really tired." I croaked this.

And they said, "Sure." And then, after a long while, Dr. Patterson came in and said, "I think I'll take you out of a lot of this." He took a large pair of scissors and cut off the outer mask. Then I could see around and I could move my head just a very little bit because I had heavy bandages on my slit throat and they had a tube in me so that I wouldn't clot. They were so afraid of blood clots. I was afraid of strangling.

The next day was just the same, but a new nurse came since the other one couldn't take it. (Where were Maas and Quigley? Other jobs. They'd thought I was safe.)

Again I sat up, struggling not to drown in my own phlegm. The following morning I was somewhat better, but my voice was gone. Absolutely gone. Now I could not even whisper in a hoarse croak. Now there was nothing but air whistling. Walter came, as always, after supper, and I simply couldn't speak to him. All I could do was look at him with sad, sad eyes from the bandages and, poor thing, who had been so faithful, so brave, so constant just lost heart. I saw him lose heart in front of me. It was one of two times. And he said, "I must go. I can't talk to you. You can't answer. And I can't be of any help and I think you're tired." And so he left and went home and called a friend and said, "I can't save her. She's going."

Well, *they* saved me and *it* saved me, whatever "it" was, and it was very hard that night and very, very tiring. And I put my head down on the discomfort and the misery and leaned against it. I was so, so tired. Weary to death. But still alive, still sentient. And I just rested on misery. One can do that, you know.

The next day in came another resident surgeon, a Dr. Piddle (not Dr. Meadows, who'd been rotated to another ward), and at twilight Piddle decided to make mud pies. I don't know what he was doing. But he got some blood, I think from the left (good) arm, and some glass slides and began playing and dabbling. He had a little spatula and he mixed it all up and made little games for himself there. And while he did this, which seemed perfectly futile, he chattered.

"I hear Dr. Patterson hurt your vocal cords." My hair stood on end.

I opened what was left of my eyes to their extreme width. "He what?" I whispered, or rather whistled, at him.

"He hurt your vocal cords. I'm not saying you won't speak again. You probably will, but it will take some time." And he went on playing and dabbling.

And that night I had *that* to cushion myself on. And the next morning—because finally the weekend was over (oh, those summer weekends!)—Dr. Patterson came in and I whistled at him, "Have you hurt my vocal cords?"

"Certainly not."

"Well, Dr. Piddle (and this, I promise you, is not his name, nor can it be traced), Dr. Piddle said you had destroyed my vocal cords."

"What nonsense!"

"You have not hurt me?"

"No."

"Is the loss of voice usual?"

"It's routine. You won't speak again for two or three days, but it means absolutely nothing but a small trauma because of the pulling and hauling of the tubes."

"I'm safe then?"

"Absolutely safe." And he said, "You're not going to have any more embolisms. None at all. They are gone. We cut it out and threw it away. It's gone."

"One thing," I whistled. "Help us. Help the patients.

Don't let Dr. Piddle deal with living people." Dr. Patterson said nothing.

Later that day Dr. Piddle came in and said, "I must have some arterial blood."

"Oh dear," I said. "That hurts."

"Yes," he said. "But not too much."

And I said, "Take the right arm. I can't feel. I'm tired of having the left arm used for arterial blood." The arteries lie well below the veins, which means that they have to go in with buttonhooks and grappling tools and fish them out. And I thought that arm didn't feel, but it did feel, only the wrong way. It didn't feel pain. It felt a nerve-racking incidence of trouble, and it was absolutely intolerable, and he couldn't get a good artery. He kept fishing and poking and hauling and he could not latch onto one. And I said, "Doctor, this is intolerable." And Maas (who'd blessedly come back) said, finally, "That's enough. You've had three tries and that's enough. She's got to rest. I think she's losing consciousness." And, indeed, I was on the point of fainting, and we sent him out of the room. And I said, as he left, "I must be told by Dr. Plum that it's necessary" and breathed heavily. And when Dr. Plum came in I whispered to him the troubles and said, "Must I have it?"

And he said, "Certainly not."

And I said, "Another thing. They tried to give me pills tonight and they were the wrong pills and I refused to take them." So the pill girl brought them in for inspection and he said, "What absolute nonsense! Criminal nonsense!" And he walked out of that room faster than I've ever seen him and I think he beheaded three or four nurses right then. It was all very quiet and very polite and the patients never knew, but it was a deadly mistake. I must say, however, that I was in the hospital three and a half months and I had upward of six to seven sets of pills a day and only one bad mistake had been made. Fortunately I recognized the fact that this was a new pill and I hadn't been forewarned and I'd better not take it, so I survived.

Now they said I was on the road to recovery. All the trouble had been cut out of me. I could get well.

My first visitor was Cy Peck of the New York *Times*, a very charming, gentle gentleman, and he was sitting talking to me benignly. He wouldn't take any alcohol and he wouldn't take any tea. He didn't take anything. He just sat there and quietly talked, and I put my hand up to my bandaged throat and it came away red and sticky. I was bleeding right through the bandages, right through all the gauzes and the sticking plaster. A hemorrhage is very secret and it's silent and it oozes and you don't know you're bleeding until you put your hand to the wound and then it's red and sticky.

I said, "You'd better get a doctor." So he did and they took one look and said, "Out," or something like that, and got to work. He offered to wait but I begged out. The doctors had to rebandage my neck and pulled all the plugs and all the wires. "Too much anticoagulant." And they put me on something else!

The next day Jerome Robbins came, looking very smart in his summery light suit and shirt, and he was extremely ebullient and we began gossiping about dance companies, etc., and he spoke of the Boston Ballet and he said, "I understand you think they're pretty good."

And I said, "Yes, I do. They're conscientious and very good and I did them a nice ballet last spring to the music of . . . to the music . . . of . . . Jerry, get the first white coat you meet and send it in to me quickly!" The first white coat that he met was Caroline McCagg, and she came in instantly and sat for the next half hour holding my hand and taking my pulse and my blood pressure every four minutes. She could see that I was terrified. I talked absolutely uncontrollable syllables and they pulled all the plugs again.

"What is my name?" said Piddle, and I looked at him and shook my head. This time it was only forty minutes before I came back to some sort of normal speech, and the doctor said, "My name is Piddle, incidentally."

And I said, "I haven't forgotten." Nor will I.

Three days later I called up Robbins and I said, "Jerry, the composer whose name escaped my memory . . ."

And he said, "Don't give it a thought. I forget names."

And I said, "I always forget names, too, but not this one." The composer's name was, as it happens, Franz Schubert.

Ten days later I said to Dr. Gorham, who had returned

from his vacation, "While you were gone I died twice and they slit my throat."

And he said, "Yes, I saw the charts."

I said, "You know, if your men would leave me alone I think I could get well." And that went down on the chart, too, and it was the talk of the floor.

A few days later they said rather smugly that they had the medication in the correct proportions, my recipe was determined, and now I would get well.

Then the next day I said, "You know something. I'm beginning to like this life very, very much and I don't want to help myself anymore. I want to be helped. And I don't want to use my right hand and I don't want to sit up and I don't want to walk."

And the next day they all came in and said, "It's time you went home." And it was.

My final memory of the hospital was of Maas standing on the sidewalk with the empty wheelchair, waving gallantly. Waving and waving till we were out of sight.

I left behind me my weaving, a table mat for Jonathan, in tasteful green and yellow wool. This was an unusual table mat. It had cost thirty-two thousand dollars.

X

INTERLUDE: DR. PLUM'S POSTOPERATIVE REFLECTION

Looking back, these final episodes seem almost trivial. But at the time we thought Agnes de Mille's troubles would never end.

Postoperatively, we had placed Miss de Mille on low but therapeutic doses of anticoagulants to try to prevent local clotting in the artery at the point where it had been repaired and to guard against a recurrence of the pulmonary embolism. The effects produced undue oozing of blood from the wound and required that we stop the anticoagulant on the third day, hoping that the clotting danger had ended. Other difficulties also arose. The two operations plus the diagnostic procedures had caused considerable blood loss. Furthermore, sick people regenerate their blood cells with abnormal slowness. The result was that by this time Agnes de Mille had developed a relatively severe anemia requiring treatment. Cautiously we transfused her with blood, always concerned about overloading her heart or reinducing the increased clotting tendency. She promptly developed mild heart failure. The day after that, attacks of brief speech blocking returned three times. In retrospect, I suspect that small clots did form on the inner, healing, surface of the recently opened artery and were drifting upstream. In any event, the heart failure was easily treated with digitalis and we cautiously restarted the anticoagulants, redoubling efforts to keep the dose of the drug between the extremes of either allowing emboli to form or producing further bleeding. Finally, this time all went well from the purely medical standpoint, but she had been through almost too much. Four days later the potentially worst complication developed. She wanted to stop trying.

Stress exerts its effects on human beings in many ways, some favorable, some unfavorable. Up to a certain point, depending on the intensity and the nature of the challenge, as well as on the individual person's inborn and acquired resources, stress acts as a biologically necessary and strengthening experience. Graded challenge evokes inquisitiveness, self-confidence and endurance, and adds an extra dimension to life as well. But sooner or later almost everyone reaches his or her breaking point in the face of what is perceived as overwhelming adversity. Examples of the phenomenon abound. During World War II, analysis of soldiers suffering from battle fatigue revealed that infantrymen, no matter what their background or physical health, rarely could continue in front-line duty after about 180 days of combat. Similarly, few airmen could continue to serve effectively after 50 to 70 missions without substantial behind-the-lines rest periods. Analyses of confessions extracted from prisoners of war or those forced to live under totalitarian rule show that person after person breaks after a relentless sequence that includes despair-producing events, alternating with enough temporary improvement to bring hope, only to have another threat destroy the glimpse of salvation. Prolonged and recurrently threatening illness similarly can tear at the human spirit until it contemplates capitulation as the only defense.

Throughout this devastating illness Agnes de Mille had shown an inspiring degree of courage and vitality in rising up and going forward from each of the successive assaults on her body. Finally, after almost three months of crawling back only to be knocked down again, she was almost ready to give up and let someone else carry the load, to let others feel sorry for her, pamper her, feed her, bathe her. She was almost ready to let the world bring her things instead of expecting her to learn to get them for herself and take them to others. The problem is well known among those who care for the very sick, badly traumatized or chronically ill. We doctors even have a name for it: we call it hospitalitis.

Agnes de Mille wasn't half-well, she wasn't even free of immediate medical danger. But the malaise that threatened her spirit was potentially far more life-limiting than

the disease that threatened her body. So George Gorham
and I made the last of this long series of uncomfortable
uncertain, groping choices. We sent her home: away from
the hospital, away from where the sick live; home, where
the healthy live. We sent her, hopefully, to the place
where anticipation for the rewards of the future would
begin to replace the dread that the past might recur.

PART TWO

Injury

Health is a dangerous situation between two maladies.
—JACQUES MARITAIN

The touch of her feet on the floor was like the best pianist's touch on a piano.
—MARIE RAMBERT

XI

"Don't fall," said the doctors. "You have sustained damage to your brain. You must not hurt your brain again."

My brain, my brain, my precious brain! A miraculous cauliflower in its bony case, marinating in my life-juices, pulsing sentience, direction, aggression into its tentacles, into its moving fringes—this was the dynamo, now a broken toy, this clock, this ME, ticking, ticking, wanting, asking, commanding, curious to see and be seen, to be guarded, to be tended, still wanting, surprised always, urgent, unquiet, wanting. When there is no more wanting, no more surprise, you can pull up the sheet. Watch out for wanting!

"It's like slime, really," said Plum.

I suppose like spittle. All this fuss over some spit! And other doctors are ecstatic and fascinated with urine or vomit. Entire new worlds open up for them. It's all in the viewpoint. John Donne wrote to his mistress, "O my

America, my new-found-land! My kingdom . . ." My spit.

And the memory. In the slime is the memory, the entire history of the race, the entire history of the life. Without memory there is no person. We really no longer exist as individuals. Wipe it away, clean it up. We lose the power of the legs or the arms, sight, hearing, speech. Beethoven is destroyed; the Curies; Leonardo; Euclid. The mind boggles. The slime quivers. Put it back. Put it back. It's been hurt. We hurt it. We are now dealing with an idiot. And in each globule of slime there is an entire history of the life. But it can be reached and it can be salvaged while it lives. One wants to save everything, throw nothing out. One attains the condition of the Collier brothers, those two old bachelors who holed up in their junk heap of a house so effectively that they died of starvation without help and the cadavers had to be blasted free of the debris.

There was nothing before me now but to get through my life. John Lennon said: "Life is what happens when you're making other plans."

I was not going to recover the old life. That had been destroyed with my body, sloughed off like a dead snakeskin. What lay ahead was unexperienced. In very truth, I was to be reborn and to face life as a baby, but with this difference: I had a recording mind.

How to begin? Well, first things first. Stay alive.

Walter had engaged the services of Pauline, a very handsome, tall Jamaican woman, stalwart, strapping, with a lovely caramel skin, great black eyes and a ravishing smile. She had worked formerly for a lady with a broken hip upstairs in our apartment building.

I had been sent home with a chest of drugs, phials and phials of them, together with a printed list of instructions, single-spaced, a full page long, giving me a daily schedule, so complicated that I had to follow my orders line by line. I begged to be taken off of the drugs because they made me sleepy, but at the moment the doctors would relinquish none.

I was very weak, delighted to be home, of course, but fatigued beyond anything I had ever known. The rest I took every afternoon turned out to be a two-hour nap which in no way affected my night's sleep, for I slept terribly hard through the night and into the morning. I, who had so looked forward to a shortened night's sleep, which was my due as an old woman and which would give me more time to do things, now had almost no time.

I wasn't very bright and, of course, this frightened me dreadfully. The thought of any recurrence of the lapses such as had taken place in the hospital grabbed my heart.

I was fuddled on waking up, and anyone who woke me did so with unforeseeable consequences. My family knew this but casual callers did not, and I was constantly on guard lest I expose myself.

I still continued to forget words now and then, and I discovered that I was forgetting names, everybody's names except those of my immediate relatives. I'd always been bad about names, but my forgetfulness now was

spectacular. And then I discovered I'd forgotten telephone numbers, every telephone number, including my
own. I wrote mine out carefully, along with my husband's
and Mary Green's, and it was as if I had never heard
them before. Then I'd forgotten how to add and subtract.
As for multiplication and division, the tables had to be
memorized all over again. I told no one out of shame.
And I would forget what I was going to say in the middle
of a phone conversation, and my intimates were patient
and said, "That's alright. Call back." It was humiliating
and annoying and it was frightening.

When I went in a taxi for medical treatments I
memorized—literally memorized, as if for a public appearance—the speech I would make to the driver on arrival. "Please give me a receipt." I had a horror of getting
to the end of the ride and not being able to remember the
word "receipt," of stuttering incoherencies.

I forgot where I put things, as with two thousand dollars' worth of American Express checks which I carefully
secreted and then couldn't find for nine months. Luckily I
wasn't going anywhere.

Well, so did the cleaning woman forget things, and so
did Pauline, and so did my husband. He tidied up because he couldn't stand the mess. And then he forgot
what he had tidied up and every day at least forty-five
minutes were spent trying to figure out where anything
was in the tidy, tidy room.

I was frightened I was not going to recover my old life,
that I was not going to get back my faculties. Indeed, I

was not going back in any way. I was going through this gray area to a new kind of life with entirely new rules and new values. The question was: Could I survive the spiritual shock as I had survived the physical one? Had I enough suppleness and resilience of spirit? Well, had I?

I was promised by the doctors bouts of desperate depression, crying jags, hopelessness, dismal soul-tearing, soul-dampening stretches, possibly a nervous breakdown (extremely able minds had had them). I knew none of this. I only wept at Paulette, my ex-cook, when she clamored for money in French, idiomatic French.

There were reasons why I didn't despair. One was the constant, vigilant love of my husband and son and sister. Every night my Walter served me dinner on a tray and sat and ate it with me. And every morning *he* got up, not I, as had been the custom, and made coffee, and we had a very friendly and delicious forty-five minutes of talk. And it was golden.

Walter was by nature a pessimist, so intense, so relentless, so enthusiastically morose as to be the stock joke of his family and office staff. When I first met him in 1942, he assured me that we were in a hundred-year war and that there really was no use fighting except as a gesture that he supposed we had to make out of stubborn pride. He had, of course, good reasons for thinking so. Japan held the Pacific and Hitler most of Europe. We were done for. No use.

When he married me in 1943 he assured me one night, after quite a few drinks, that he was certain he'd be killed, else he should not have become engaged or gone through with the wedding. When I showed him the script of *Oklahoma!*, his one comment as he put it down was, "Are you kidding?" When our son was born he remarked, quietly, "Well, he's just in time for the next one." His comments at my dress rehearsals had better not be repeated. But the last one was unanswerable. He came back and said, "Well, I really do think this is the worst two hours I have spent in my life." Unfortunately, he was right. He often is. Every cloudless, dazzling sky fills him with gloom. "A weather breeder," he says, looking at the flawless firmament and shaking his head.

During my illness, however, he had been quietly patient, and every time I had said, "I don't know what I'll do," all he said was, "Not for long; it won't last. This is not permanent." And I held on to his faith as the drowning hold on to a stick. He never varied, not once, in my presence. He never wavered.

"Walter," I said quite soberly one morning over coffee, "I do not want to labor this point, because it's meaningless in a sense and needs no repetition, but I want to tell you that I'm sorry for what I've done to your life. I am very, very sorry." And he looked at me mildly and said quietly, "My dear, this has been the making of me."

Friends didn't expect him to behave with such dedication. Indeed, can anyone *expect* such discipline and continuing unselfishness? He merely opened his eyes wide at their surprise. "I didn't think. It was perfectly natural.

She needed me." The strength was there. The love was there when we needed it. He didn't have to think.

Another reason for hope was my project, my book. This was a source of strength to me such as I cannot possibly overstate. It didn't matter whether it was a good book or a bad book. It was my book and it was lovely for me to think about because it dealt with my extreme youth, when everything was beginning. There was a healing in all these memories.

And the third reason for courage was the enormous friendship, the flowers, the letters, the letters which came without letup, on and on, even after the hospital. We were now going into the fourth month after the stroke and still the flowers came. One kind friend sent an enormous arranged bouquet every week for ten weeks. My wardrobe mistress wrote me three times a week, cards, notes, whatever. And another couple of friends sent cards two or three times every week. In the hospital they began and it continued after. They didn't phone. Now and then they phoned Mary Green. Everyone phoned Mary Green just for bulletins. They never disturbed me. Nor Walter.

My immediate objective was not to be a nuisance in daily ways. A burden I was—and would remain—and there was no use gilding it over with fine language. I was a helpless cripple and I was going to be a trouble. There was nothing I could do about that. I and my family had to face it together. But I could try desperately hard not to be a constant, hourly bother. I could try not to be so dependent.

"Don't be so helpless," said the doctors. "Use your hand." Use it? My God! Well, I tried. I'd put it in my eye. I'd put it up through my cheek. I'd put it down the front of my dress. I spilled. I dropped. They tied towels around me at table. Much later, when I went marketing with Pauline, she gave me things to hold and I held them with my unconscious right hand while I ferreted through the shelves with my left, and then I would find preserved peaches and pickles and beans and shards of glass all on the floor, all broken. A neighbor, seeing me sitting in my wheelchair in Gristede's with the broken glass and the remnants of brandied peaches at my feet, wept in pity. I looked busy and contented; I hadn't known anything had fallen. After a time I stopped marketing; it didn't seem to help the household any.

I could carry nothing with liquid from one room to the next. I could not even carry a book because the left hand was taken up with a tri-pronged stick I used for walking.

I learned certain limitations. Do precisely one thing at a time, *one thing*. I learned this like an exercise. Any normal person can rise, turn the head and look, stretch out a hand and take up an object in a single count; now it cost me five very slow counts: rise, look, settle cane, establish balance and take up object with left hand; then, if I had to walk with an object, a new set of problems presented themselves, sometimes involving ingenuity and teeth, and all requiring time and an absorption with trivia; the inchworm's point of view.

I learned never to stoop down, to lean over or swivel around without first taking my glasses off. Putting my hand up to my head to keep the glasses in place had been second nature. Now, of course, not. It held a cane. I couldn't use the right, not if I valued my eyes. I had to think ahead. This was brand new. Everything had to be placed where a mistake could not be made. I learned never to look away from what I was doing. I phoned once and put the phone back on the bedside table and then discovered my right hand was resting comfortably in a bowl of sour cream. Well, why not?

I used to hit my husband in the face at night. How could I help it? I didn't know the arm had moved. I didn't know where the arm was! He learned to sleep while shading his eyes, and he would say in the middle of the night, "Hey! Watch it!" And then I would be very sorry. I learned to keep the right hand safely inactive by holding it with the left whenever I was with anyone else, because I wished to keep it out of trouble and because I didn't want to lose track of it as I sometimes did in bedclothes or under papers. One night I grabbed the hand and took it under the covers and said, "There now. You be good. You stay quiet. You stay warm and quiet." And I put it on my breast. And that was fine except it wasn't my hand.

My hand became known as Creepie and my husband always referred to it as male. One night he said, "You aren't paying enough attention to Creepie. You're not taking care of him. If you're not nice to Creepie I'll take over. Creepie and I have a life together you know nothing about." And I said, "Walter, I think that is probably the most obscene remark I ever heard."

What I learned fairly quickly and had never known before, although I had lived with it all my life, was the simple fact of tactile recognition. We know where our hands are and where our arms are because we feel where they are, because of the unending series of radar signals from the extremities. Now I was without these signals and I didn't know.

It was fortunate that I had spent all my adult life with physical discipline. Not only did I know how to follow instructions, I also knew—and this is important—how long it would take to expect a response. I know a great deal about the practical use of muscles; for instance, how long it takes to build them and how quickly they deteriorate. Dancers who rest for two weeks are completely out of order when they resume. But even I was surprised that in two months, in three and a half months in the hospital bed I could lose entirely the right leg and thigh, so that they were wasted and thinner, so that the muscles atrophied. And, of course, there was no feeling. Such a deterrent! But I do know that these muscles regrow with effort and use. They do regrow. Nerves do not.

Fatiguing? Wasteful? Yes indeed. But also sporting.

I must not be exasperated or out of patience. I recognized that adults go to the most troublesome and expensive lengths to give themselves play hurdles to surmount.

And here I was with a dial telephone in my hand and I had the same problems quite free.

Try to dial a telephone with the claw that I used or put on the TV with a hook, with one dancing finger, one frenzied stick. When I finally was able to put the TV on, reach the lever and press it down, it was for me a hole in one. The other hand was always, of course, engaged in holding me up, supporting and balancing me, and seeing that I did not crash down and start the internal bleeding that the doctors never ceased to warn me about.

I couldn't bring my husband a cup of coffee, but there were other things I had to learn to do, had to for the dignity of the house and for my relations with my husband. The Broken Hip lent us her wheelchair and her commode, which Walter established beside my bed at night. I have never before used my husband as a trained nurse. Now I was forced to. I didn't like it. "My darling," he said, "this is a very little thing to do for you and it's only temporary." But I didn't like it. It meant, among other things, waking him up every time I wanted to use the commode, and he needed his sleep because he worked very hard. So one night I attempted to get up alone in the dark. The commode was only a foot away but I fell. And then, of course, he had to wake up and pick me up between the commode and the bed as I lay in a crumple. And that was rather difficult because I simply couldn't remember which leg to push up on. And he had to lift me with prodigious effort from the floor, dead weight. The next night I attempted to do better, but still in the dark.

(Remember, I couldn't feel.) And I took hold of the book-stand by my bed and I lost my balance and teetered and brought the entire construction over on top of me: a lamp, two telephones, water, notebooks, all my books. The crash and the confusion were loud and disturbing, and after he had unearthed me and I had righted myself by the side of the bed, he said, "I really can't change the whole bed. It's sopping wet down this side. You'll have to lie on the other and lie very still." And that's the way I finished the night. By the third night the cleaning woman and Pauline had purchased a night-light and rigged it up so that I could control it with the left hand.

The next objective was to learn to go all the way across the room to the bathroom: waking up all muddled, all directionless and grabbing the three-pronged stick and tottering off across the rug and through the door and into the bathroom, which, of course, had a tile floor and hard edges to the tub and toilet. (And I must not fall. And I must not bump myself.) Well, I did it.

Now, this seems like nothing when I say it. I once was able easily to do 144 relevés, 64 fouetté pirouettes, and hold prolonged balances on full point. But that trip to the bathroom, which, of course, became my habitual path, was as big an achievement. And it also involved terror, which the ballet stunts did not.

I remember in my son's infancy he had to spend time in a hospital. There was a very young baby, about a week old, who had been born without an anus. The surgeons made him a new one. And the mother hung over the crib

watching to see what would happen with the first passage
of fecal matter. And it all worked. The entire apparatus
worked and she almost slipped to her knees. The Brooklyn Bridge was a tremendous achievement, and the first
people who crossed it knew an experience no one ever
had before, but this child made history because where
nothing had worked and where before he was doomed, he
now worked.

My trip to the bathroom in privacy and decency meant
more to me than a rave notice in the New York *Times*.

After I had been home two or three days, the therapists, who had been balked and were chafing, gathered
like terrier pups and said, "Let's have at you!" Poor frus-
trated things. No sooner had they got a good trend under
way than I had been snatched from them in total collapse
and forbidden by the doctors to move at all. Dr. McCagg,
who was, of course, a licensed doctor, and knew exactly
what was wrong with me, understood. The others did not.

Caroline McCagg explains:

"Because her hospitalization had been so prolonged,
with one major life-threatening problem after another, no
one wanted to recommend further in-patient rehabilitation, and my feeling was that we could work out a
home program that would be adequate. The disadvantage
of doing it this way was that it took longer, but, more
significantly, it took much more emotional energy on her
part. She had much less help from the cadre of experts
who can simplify and streamline the mundane problems
of everyday living. I do not think that any other patient I

have ever had or ever will have could have done what she did." (Dr. McCagg's experience had been limited to ordinary people; any trained ballet dancer would have behaved as I did, or even more industriously.)

"It was the hard way. Maybe I should have started her in an in-patient, formal rehab program, but at that time I felt that she would not be able to put up with the in-flexible, cookie-cutter approach to disability; nor was she physically strong enough to tolerate hours of therapy. I felt strongly also that she needed some period of con-valescing in the security of familiar surroundings."

I didn't know until later that I had been on a hairline division between extreme agony and the void where I practiced my tightrope. By the grace of God—and I mean this in all piety—by the grace of God I was spared pain.

Gerry, the darling, jolly girl, came down to my house after her hospital hours accompanied by, if you please, Caroline McCagg herself to see where I could practice. The therapy was one of the ways toward some sort of usefulness. I walked on Gerry's arm down the hall once and nearly fainted. She couldn't believe it, but it was true. And then she started giving me exercises for my arm. The right arm had stiffened up and calcified in some morbid way, so that if I raised it or swung it, it hurt most abominably. And she had to freeze it with ice packs be-fore she could get to work massaging and forcing me to build up the wasted muscles.

"Why ice?" I said. "Why not heat?"

"Very simple," she answered. "You can't feel if I burn

you." After about fifteen or twenty minutes of freezing I was able to move the arm and shoulder some inches. The leg was ridiculously different. It moved alright, but it wouldn't hold and I couldn't keep it straight in any direction. It wavered and dropped with a will of its own. I had no control over my pretty leg. My point. Gone wild!

I found out one very useful fact that most people will not have to learn, although some will: One can learn other controls.

If you can't feel the foot, if you can't feel the knee but you can feel the hip, you can control your foot and knee from the hip. I could straighten my knee by controlling the thigh. I could hold my arm unwavering in the air through the shoulder. I had never lost any sensation in the shoulder. One holds up a hand, but my hand was beyond help, undisciplined and undiscovered. So, by gum, the shoulder would have to do all the work. Little by little it did. You have to concentrate very hard, but it can be done.

When I was a child starting ballet lessons, I had a fantasy which pleased me very much: I used to play with the idea of what would happen if I were given Pavlova's body without her knowledge or her art—I would retain my own —but her leg, her thigh, her back and her arms. Would I be able to dance as she did or would I use this golden instrument with the skill of a five-year-old beginner picking at a Stradivarius? I think now that I probably would be able to dance a little like Pavlova. The knowledge lies in the muscles and in the habit of the muscles. Every dancer knows that in trying to remember ballet roles long after the conscious mind has given up all recollection, the memories come back as one starts to move in the old patterns and to the familiar music. It does not seem to be conscious. The patterns work themselves out through habit, apparently through the muscles. This is a very curious but universally recognized phenomenon as long as the muscular memory remains intact. But mine had been destroyed.

For this reason, although right-handed, I gave up trying to write with the right hand. For when I inserted a pen in the right-hand fingers, it was as though I had never held a pen in my life—curious and strange. While I thought right-handed and right control of the pencil, my right-hand fingers itched to begin. I simply could not manage it. All the knowledge in the mind remained in the mind, but the knowledge in the muscles and in the reflexes had been totally obliterated. So I gave up the right. I must admit I did. I learned to write with the left, not quickly but legibly.

The therapists thought it would be a fine idea, since I used to be a pianist, for me to start to play the piano again. Of course I didn't expect to attack the "Black-Key Etude" right off, but I did expect my fingers to stay on the keyboard. What a hope! My hand hit air.

Nor did I practice my therapy as Gerry wished. She ordered about twenty minutes four times a day and I did nothing of the sort. She had looked upon everything medical that had happened as an irritating interruption hardly to be tolerated or forgiven. Now she was ready for real work, hours of it, and daily.

But equally with the body I had to keep my mind in some sort of order. I had to, or I would stop wanting to live. Gerry accepted this theory, but she didn't really understand. Keeping my mind in some sort of order meant that I worked at my book and that I learned to write my checks left-handed and that I learned to talk, and other things which took time and attention. And that was, in a way, time stolen from the legs and arms. So it was stolen.

Walter used to get very irritated with me. "Have you practiced your therapy? Twice? Three times? Have you?" Well, no, I hadn't. "If you're not good about this," he would scold, "I will send you to the Rusk Institute. I will banish you." And I must say the thought of that brought tears to my eyes.

I had known nothing about how sick I was when I came home. I had not understood because I had not been told about the anemia, the need for blood transfusions, the heart failure, or the various other distressing aberrations which dismayed the doctors. I knew nothing at all about them until I read Dr. Plum's notes in February of 1981—six years after the events—and I must confess I was shocked.

Walter knew. Walter knew all about the responsibility of taking me home and how very sick I was, and he was nervous and apprehensive; and so indeed was Jonathan. They rehearsed all they had to do—getting me into the car, getting me out of the car, taking me in the elevator upstairs, taking me around the apartment—all of that, and he was watchful, considerate and solicitous with the utmost compassion.

But at the same time he adopted a course of teasing me, like a football coach, toward health, cheering me through the exercises, baiting me to try in all daily matters. Try harder, try better. Use my hand, use my leg and foot, use my body to the point of extreme fatigue. Well, that didn't take long. But it was very wearing and he was seemingly unthinking, unperceiving. This was an erroneous impression, but I believe he understood that if he let up on me for one day, I would slide back little by little toward absolute sloth. There was every inclination to do so, so he persisted with the dogged determination of a trained nurse. Oh, no. More with the determination of a trained coach. More with the passion of a devotee. Have you done your exercises today? All of them? Have you walked around the block? (Around the block? Good God!) Try to walk up the stairs. Try to walk without the cane. Try. And then there would be a joke, because his humor was extraordinary. Whatever he said, no matter how terribly forceful or nagging, there was always wonderful wit, and I laughed and he laughed. Without this tireless nagging toward effort, I think I would not have recovered, or not have recovered so well. I owe him survival.

But now I was home and I wanted to stay home. I also wanted to keep my mind. Couldn't they understand that?

And that meant, of course, my enthusiasm. That miraculously had not flagged.

Eventually Gerry went off to California seeking her fortune. McCagg changed hospitals, switching to the Columbia Presbyterian way up at 168th Street, an unwieldy distance. All her good girls drifted away. That is when Natalie Stelzer came to me, who has been with me ever since. She used to arrive on a bicycle from Brooklyn.

The doctors said, "Get out. Walk up and down the street."

I have been talking about walking. I didn't walk, I inched. The sensation was, and is, exhausting and to a certain extent, painful.

Gerry used to say, "Take a long walk down to the corner." Gerry, of course, was a roughrider. Pauline helped me down to the street in my wheelchair and I took my pronged tripod and I started out. Shuffle. Close. Shuffle. Close. With pain, with exhaustion and, yes, with fear. As far as the laundry door. As far as the cleaner's door. As far as the first stairway. Don't take your eyes off the pavement. If you fall you will bruise yourself and you may bleed to death. Once, years before the hemorrhage, when I was walking smartly (in a moderate heel) along Riverside Drive and gazing not at where I was going but at the really astonishing old architecture, I stepped into a hole and plunged, turning my ankle. The pain was so stunning that I lay for appreciable seconds with my eyes closed. I opened them to find a woman and a little boy staring at me.

"Are you alright?" asked the woman helpfully.

"Certainly, madame," I replied. "I lie here every afternoon. I find it rests me."

I fell all the time, but in those days there was no injury.
Now it was dangerous.

These days Pauline brought the chair right behind me
and I was allowed to rest. Two days later try the next
house. Two days later the house beyond. It was hot. It
was painful. Oh, well, heavens! I did it. Others have done
more.

When I say there was pain, let me try to be explicit.
When the normal person feels pain, he or she identifies it
instantly with the cause: I am cut, I am bruised, I am
burnt, I am mashed. What I felt was always a great fatigue in the left leg, because it took the burden of my
weight and effort, and in the right a constant tingling,
burning sensation. At quiet moments this was in abeyance
and I disregarded it. But when I stopped for a moment to
think about it, it was there, a hot, burning feeling. Under
stress this became intensified enormously. With effort it
augmented considerably: greater burning, greater tingling, until it approached the pain threshold. But what
made it very difficult was that I could not ever identify
the source or even the exact region afflicted; so my foot
burned, let me say painfully, for want of another word
comprehensible enough. I could not tell if it was a wrinkle in the stocking, an oppressive weight, or stubbing or
crushing. I could not have told if I were being burnt. The
sensation of pressure on the nerve ends was excruciating,

out of all proportion to what I felt on the other side, and the fatigue was therefore hard to bear because there was the element of mystery and apprehension in every situation; for example, a slight contact of the toe would be felt in the groin. One time I got my foot caught in the car door. In this case I really felt nothing, but the door wouldn't close. I'm very surprised I did not break the bones in the toes. I have felt as much discomfort from having a wrinkle in my stocking. In that case I would have to stop and remove my shoe and then the stocking—all with the left hand—or get somebody to help me. Humiliating, tedious and peculiar.

Once on the street a woman stopped me, a stranger, young, gentle, and said, "My dear, what is happening to your right leg?"

Ah, if she but knew!

"Look," she said.

I looked down very slowly and carefully, and there was a stocking trailing two or three feet behind me.

She said, "May I?" and knelt and tried to yank it away and couldn't, it being somehow attached to me. So she knelt in the filth and tucked it up around my leg and fastened it and pulled the trouser leg down and said, "Can't go 'round like that, you know. Besides, you'll trip yourself."

And she made me tidy until I could get indoors and rectify the trouble. It devolved that I had put on my panty hose with another stocking caught up in it, which trailed down now through the trouser leg about a yard.

And not being able to feel, I knew nothing about it. But she took the trouble and the time and the care. This kind of solicitude I found frequently.

As with crossing the street. Later, when I attempted to do this alone, never looking up, trusting that the vehicles obeyed the traffic signals, there was always someone quickly at my elbow, usually a woman but not always, proffering help very kindly.

The first time I went to a shop alone (which was our corner flower store) they gave me a small box of roses and then tied it to my wrist so that I could get home with it. I have lost so many beautiful objects because I couldn't feel when the hand opened or the fingers let go.

Once I shut my right hand in a drawer. I had put my hip against the drawer and pushed it closed, that being the only way I could get enough strength to shut it, and I was stuck there, unable to open the drawer, screaming for attention and help. That hurt. Another time I sat down on a chair without looking (fatal, forbidden mistake! Every therapist warns and warns and warns). But I did, feeling the chair just behind me, but I didn't know exactly where it was and I overbalanced, since I had feeling in only one buttock, and fell heavily, cracking my head against the desk. I was slightly dazed and very frightened. Pauline got me on the bed and applied cold cloths. All was well, nothing to worry about. I proceeded to my dinner table— at which, I am happy to say, Dick Cavett was the honored guest—and I had a fine time. But pain started in the right wrist and I thought, "Oh goodness, I'm getting arthritis! Well, at my age who can wonder?" The pain increased. The next morning my arm was badly swollen and blue. I had fallen on the wrist in some way without knowing it and the hand and arm were damaged (not broken) without my having any idea that I had done anything but give my noggin a thwack.

I once sat down incorrectly on the toilet seat (it is of these small, vulgar and daily happenings that our lives are now made) and sustained a bruise. In two days the bruise was the size of a baseball. In four days my leg was black from below the knee to the groin. I am not speaking in hyperbole. I do not mean purple-black or green-black. I mean black and very sensitive and sore. It looked like gangrene. I went to the hospital and a substitute doctor said to me, "Dear, dear, this is serious. You must take your Coumadin carefully, always." And I said, "Do I have to keep taking Coumadin for the rest of my life?" And he said, "Alas, yes." The next day I went to my own doctor and he said, "We'll take you off Coumadin this afternoon. Obviously too much." Well, medicine is supposed to be a fairly exact science. The left leg and thigh were so sore that for eight months I could not do my regular daily exercises of stretching. That was the good leg.

I went for an examination at the Rusk Institute and Dr. Sarno said, "Rise up on your toes. Put your arms around my neck and rise up." And so I did, in my peculiar way; that is, I rose on the left toe and trusted that the right was following suit. And then he said, "Try to rise on the right toe." Nothing. Flannel. I pushed and pushed. Relevés

onto full point? I, who had an ankle of steel? Cotton wool.
"Let it go," he said. "Let it go. That's past. You won't get
that back." His remark stung me. In two months I was
doing four relevés and in six months I was doing eight. It
is not just the weakness and nonfeeling that is frustrating.
It is the terrible weight of the rest of the body: the
weight of the leg, which seems to pull about ninety-five
pounds by itself, and the weight of the arm, which seems
to weigh about forty-five pounds. And not only that but,
in the case of the arm, a restraint like a heavy band.
Bondage. Pushing against gravity as with the leg. Pushing
to inertia. You deal with gravity every time you do anything at all, even putting your hand to your head. But let
me say to those who need to know, keep trying. Under
doctors' supervision, of course, keep trying. Lie back and
pant. But keep trying.

"I seemed, however, to have little aptitude for the business," I wrote long ago. "What had all this talk about
God-given talent amounted to? I seemed to be all rusted
wire and safety pins. It was like trying to wiggle my ears.
I strained and strained. Nothing perceptible happened. A
terrible sense of frustration drove me to striving with
masochistic frenzy. Twice I fainted in class."

This is a quotation from my first book, *Dance to the
Piper*, concerning my first ballet lessons and the training
of a young, uncouth body into the extraordinarily difficult
disciplines of the balletic style. And here I was, fifty-odd
years later, doing it all over again. But this time with
what impediments and handicaps! In the first instance

long ago, I would try to point a toe and there were no muscles and there was no sensation and I had to force and force, through muscle, through wood. But then I had been able to feel the ends of my foot tapping on the floor. This time I could feel nothing, and this time I knew how to apply the pressures and the energies. So I strained on the instep, on the toe muscles, on the calves, on the knee, on the thigh, and still there was no sensation. I saw in the mirror the foot move a half inch, but there was no sensation, and therefore there was no satisfaction of any kind. The body was not pleasured with fulfillment of effort. Nevertheless I had to continue to practice. It was, when you got right down to it, a bloody bore, and it would have to be done every day.

After a bit, I got a real ballet barre put up in the back room and there I practiced not pliés, grands battements, or développés but walking steps, forward and back, forward and back. "Walking equivalents," they're called. Don't let the instep go! Don't let the foot turn over. You'll kill yourself if you do. Difficult but getting easier. And then kneeling, watching in the mirror, sitting down on the soles of my feet. The pain at first was rending. I could not squat on my soles Japanese style, the easiest sit in the world. Who had shriveled up my hamstrings? Who had tightened them into little knots? Shortened them? Demeaned them? Don't whimper. Stretch them. Stretch them. Make it happen. And then, sitting on the floor, try to put the head down between the knees till it touches the floor. Do it. Do it. First once. Then twice. Then five times. And then a few more, and let the cheek rest on the ground. And the pain on the left was real pull and stretch. And the pain on the right was altogether different.

It occurred to me at some point that I would have to learn these different pains. I did have sensations in the right foot and in the right leg—nothing that made any sense to me, nothing that was related to my previous experience—but they were sensations, and as people learned telegraphic signals or light signals or flag signals, I must learn pain signals. I suppose little children learn these when they're just beginning. They don't know what's hot and what's cold, what's harmful and what is safe. They have to find out. I must learn the tingling that meant I had a wrinkle in my stocking as opposed to the tingling that meant someone was standing on my foot. There was no difference in intensity, but there was, I was sure, a slight difference in the tingling.

Scientists have recently devised a method of recording the movement of fish with tones, and the tunes (if you can call them that), while not exactly catching, are piquant. They do, however, record the fish. Surely I could learn to read back my own tones. I would learn them at the barre. Patience first, and attention and discipline and the satisfaction of knowing that with will and patience one could do almost anything. The barre was my rope of life as it has been the salvation of every dancer.

But I was not properly faithful. I failed through my inertia, through hopeless ennui. There are those who keep going, through faith, without reward or pay. When one remembers the biblical adage, "For the laborer is worthy of his hire," this has nothing to do with us. We were worthy of our effort and that was all.

Oh, but I was lucky! I had my speech, hearing, and eyes. But there were, however, aspects to the situation that disturbed and irritated me constantly, and I will list them because I do not think unhurt people, as a rule, tend to think about them.

Do not take for granted that patients are feebleminded unless they are. Do not take for granted that because they can't speak quickly they cannot think either quickly or adequately. Frequently they can, and your impatience, which is a modern trait, will only frustrate and confuse them. Learn a little patience yourself. It won't hurt you. They have had to learn an entirely new tempo for the whole of their lives and they cannot speak quickly no matter what your exigency.

Do not supply helpful substitutes for hesitant or slow words—that is, if you have any interest in determining precisely what the patient wants. You may possibly not have. Then go ahead, make up your own conversation. Nurses, friends and passersby used to speak about me in the third person, as though I were not present, and offer suggestions as to what I wanted while I vainly tried to make myself heard. They never addressed me directly. It was universal, I repeat, universal to demand information or corroboration from my paid employees while I sat quite able to speak for myself. This was done in the name

of helpfulness and sympathy. It was really in the name of
impatience.

VERBATIM EXAMPLE

SCENE: Beauty parlor. Agnes (A) sits with large bib
draped around her, hair, like white fleece, is combed out.
An elderly male operator (O) hovers anxiously. A dryer is
whining con fuoco fortissimo.

A. (trying to raise her weak voice) Please fasten the
hair at the back, attach the hairpiece and comb my own
hair into large rolls to meet the hairpiece.

(O. picks up a handful of bobby pins.)

A. Don't use bobby pins. I can't manage them with
one hand. Fasten the hair with an elastic.

O. With a what?

A. An elastic.

O. What is that?

A. You can't hear me. Come down here.

(His face is brought close for one, one and a half
counts. He straightens. He is busy.)

A. An elastic.

O. We don't have any.

A. A beauty parlor without an elastic?

O. We've never had one.

A. Oh, drat the noise of that dryer! You can't hear me.

O. I can.

(He is busy.)

A. Don't use bobby pins. I've brought hairpins. Look.

O. I can't use those.

A. Try, please.

O. No, I can't.

(His mouth is full of bobby pins. He can't hear. He sticks them in like pins in a cushion.)

A. I can't manage bobby pins.

(He clamps the hairpiece on the back and pins it flat.)

A. This is not going to hold. Look.

(A. pulls out all the loose strands of her own white hair, handfuls of them. He throws down the brush angrily and is gone. He is replaced by a young Japanese girl [J.G.], quite lovely and obviously smart.)

A. Please don't use bobby pins.

J.G. I'm going to get a rubber band.

A. A rubber . . . Ahhh, I understand.

(The hair is snapped into place.)

A. That's fine. Now curl my own hair over the hairpiece. Pin the hairpiece low. Please don't use . . . never mind.

(The hair is fastened high up and my own hair is secured on top in a tight, hard bun.)

A. You can't hear me. You don't understand. Please come low. This dryer makes it impossible for you to hear me.

J.G. I hear you.

A. Bring your face close.

(She holds it for one, two and a half counts. She is busy. She turns away. She is gone. She is pinning. The hair is high. My own hair is plastered into a knot, like a turd.)

A. I don't want my hair fastened like that.

(She starts to pull it out.)

J.G. Take your hand away. I can't work with your hand . . .

A. I don't want . . .

J.G. Don't do that. Don't interfere with me.

(She restrains the wrist in both her hands.)

A. You must listen to me.

J.G. I hear you. Don't.

(She all but slaps the hand. The dryer suddenly stops. There is silence.)

A. Thank God. Now listen. Pin the hairpiece lower on my head and pin the loose hair, my own, in soft rolls around it.

(J.G. does so.)

A. Keep it low.

J.G. I'm keeping it low.

(The hair is high.)

A. Oh, God.

(A. turns to a neighbor.)

A. Can you help me?

N. It's lovely, dear. She did a lovely job. You should be very pleased.

(Japanese attendant has gone into an opaque stillness.)

A. I look like Martha Mitchell.

(Silence)

A. Do you know who Martha Mitchell is?

N. (Helpfully) She wrote Clark Gable's book. She wrote *Gone With the Wind*.

A. I don't like this.

(Japanese girl exits. Elderly owner of shop [E.O.S.] comes up.)

E.O.S. What is it, dear? Tell me what you want.

A. Well . . .

E.O.S. But this is lovely. This is perfectly lovely. Here's a mirror.

(She flashes it at the back of A.'s head.)

A. I couldn't see. Bring it back.

(E.O.S. grinds teeth, rolls eyes and brings it back.)

A. No.

E.O.S. It looks lovely, you know. We can see. You can't see.

(Both go off to prepare the bill. A.'s head, under its towering mass of curls, false hair and bobby pins, sinks low. In the unusual silence voices cut through. Echo from across the shop.)

J.G. If she'd only say what she wants.

E.O.S. Poor thing! You've got to be patient.

J.G. Jesus! I am, but she doesn't say what she wants.

E.O.S. We must forgive her. (To Pauline, coming to fetch A.) You should have stayed. She can't explain.

J.G. You'd think it made a difference anyway how she looks. I mean, well, *you* know what I mean.

Do not help physically unless you are told just how, what to grab and what to push. Do not give any physical

help at all unless you are appealed to, and then listen
carefully to find out how it must be offered. Generally it
will take no strength. If it requires strength, you will be
told how to offer it. There are medical ways of pulling,
lifting and supporting that do not hurt the individual aid-
ing or the patient. Do not take an arm, for instance, and
suddenly lift up. You can throw the patient quite off balance and flat on the ground in jig time. The invalid always knows which foot to place first, how to assemble
balance, how to control it and where the motor impulses
come from. Since I had no sensation whatever in the right
side, any seizure of my right arm merely put stress on the
right side, but no guidance or support. What was needed
for me (except in the bathtub) was not strength but
steadiness. Not many people can give a steady, quiet arm.
They stiffen up and try to give enough strength to lift a
paving stone. Men are better than women—and not because of strength; most women wobble.

Be careful about sudden accostings.

I could feel nothing whatever with my right foot, so I
therefore had to watch the ground and the pavement
with unceasing vigilance, no two squares of pavement in
New York City being alike and presenting as many pit-
falls as a rocky mountain path. My attention was therefore down. Children, particularly, are a hazard. They
don't, of course, look where they are going. They walk in
circles. They walk backward. They revolve, flail and zig-
zag before they notice they have turned, and after they
have turned, when they see, it is too late. Any good,

strong bump could fell me. The adolescents walking, chattering, playing transistors, with looped arms and with the most extraordinary parabolas, enchanted with the mere action of progression ensemble to noise—they accommodate no one. The mature and middle-aged walk stolidly with their eyes glued on the shop windows, turning aside never. While I was in the chair I was more or less safe, because it takes a very strong adult to knock down a chair and an occupant. But once I was out of the chair I was exposed, and I used to freeze when I saw the young approaching—freeze and pray, or try to reach the protection of a wall. Indeed, sidewalks are not safe for pedestrians.

Well-meaning friends zero in with salutations and greetings that are aimed with target precision at my bent head. They see but I don't and am not prepared.

The laundry man stands in front of me, a dear person who'd been very friendly always. He has a sack on his shoulder. "How nice to see you. You're looking well. How's Jonathan?" What I think he really means, of course, is, "Are you alive? Are you in pain? Are you going to be able to live and walk?"

"Hello." I can't look up, naturally. I am on a bad crack. I have to stop, get my balance and turn around and answer. Naturally my friend thinks I am a little slow in the head! Brain damage!

"Hi there!" This is in mid-traffic. I can't look around. I can't take my eyes from the pavement. "Agnes, it's

Dorothy!" I can't look around even if it is God Almighty.
When I get to the other side she's gone away, hurt.

"Hi there!" Someone has grabbed me from behind. I
clutch Pauline and burst into tears.

"Oh, I'm sorry. Have I hurt you? What is wrong?"

What is wrong? Oh, Jesus, what is wrong? Don't touch
me suddenly on the right side. I cannot feel and all I
know is a push. You could have taken off my arm or half
my head. Whatever you're doing, don't.

The salutation has diverted to a nervous apology. I
stand shaking, Pauline steadying me.

That's the way it was and that's the way it is.

Be sporting about the patient's limitations. Anything
put outside of the range of vision was just that, out of vision and therefore lost. It needed to be shoved but an
inch. Do it in pity's name and think to do it.

The most galling frustration for me was to lie in bed
and see what had to be straightened or picked up or tidied
—and I knew that it would not be unless I gave specific
commands. So I lived in the mess and pretended that I
didn't see the way they didn't see. It matters to me very
much that towels don't match, that cups don't match, that
wrong dishes are used, that pictures hang crooked. Well,
it's not very important, so I learned to disregard all these
things. It's a very small pleasure at best to have them in
order.

Now a word of advice to the patients.
Don't be a pig.

You will have to make choices of what to ask. You can't ask for everything. The fact that you can't walk is too damn bad, but it's nobody's fault and it doesn't mean that the people around you have to do penance. Up to this moment you have been in a situation where all adults, trained or just willing and kind, have given their entire attention and concentration to your well-being and your comfort; where every wish, as far as possible, could be gratified, and very nearly as you voiced the wish or indicated it, sometimes indeed previsioning you; and now you have to rejoin the human race and step into life. Of course you are crippled. Of course you are somewhat helpless and are therefore to be pitied and cared for. Your friends will do this. But they have also to get on with their own business, and you are not to impede them. You are *not* to. And this means discipline on your part, sharp and vigilant. Life does not stop because of you, although it is hard to evaluate the drastic change in the situation. It has occurred. You will lie for perhaps hours, waiting to express a want, and when your husband or your son come into the house at last, you're not simply to explode with demands, like a child that has been waiting to be taken to the bathroom. After a week or two of this kind of peremptory ordering, my husband said to me one night, "Would you let me get my coat off and sit down and take a breath before you start demanding?" Naturally I had been waiting for the things I wanted, and some of them were important to me. But I had to realize that he, too, had been exasperated and worn out with clamorings of every sort.

He had come in from the office and had made a long sub-
way trip and was fatigued. "I need"—I began every time
he was about to sit down.

You think of yourself as a paragon of patience, forbear-
ance, consideration. Probably not. "You were," said my
son, "pretty obnoxious." You see, this is your first experience of being helpless in a normal household. You have
been quick, thinking on your feet, planning two steps
ahead, noticing untidiness, dying flowers, dropped news-
papers. Your servants may not be quick. They probably
do not know the house and they are certainly not you.
Don't bark out so many orders that they may be immobilized and have to sit down and pull themselves together before they can act intelligently. Don't be inces-
sant and don't expect things to be done as fast as you
think of them. I expected just this. I demanded it.

Don't fret your son. You'll find he's not around much.
Don't, for instance, always conform to your own schedule
or your whims. You've suffered and you treat yourself like
a spoiled darling due for much comforting. You can get
damn nerve-racking. If Mag telephoned mid-afternoon
she likely interrupted a nap and got a befuddled wreck
confused by sleep and drugs; if she called at six she interrupted the news and got short and irritated replies; if she
called later she broke in on my time with Walter. "Oh,
my," the poor thing wailed, "I can never be right! I'm always interrupting!" I have this cry to remember. Dear
Mag, interrupt me now!

In short, Jonathan was quite right. I was obnoxious.

Finally—and this is very difficult—you must realize that your situation is changing. No matter how slowly, it is changing. You will become more independent week by week. You will become more able and you must push yourself to do for yourself as far as you can, no matter how exhausting, no matter how troublesome. The tendency will be to take for granted that you can't because up to now you haven't been able to. You must not rest in this concept. You *must* get out of bed if you can. You must walk across the room if you can. You must fetch and try to lift with care, naturally (you know your own dreadful limitations). But you must keep trying. This will be exhausting. But you must if you are to have relationships with the people around you. I cannot warn more urgently on this point. There are patients—and every doctor knows them—who simply lie back on the bed of roses and say, "I can't. I will not. Help!" And they're bloody bores and they become a tyrannical drag on their families. They will be avoided when possible. That's the healthy reaction and that's exactly what they will get.

And, ultimately, don't always talk about yourself as in this book. People are curious and will say they are deeply interested, but they truly are not. In the first place, they cannot comprehend what you are telling them. Second, they feel inadequate to respond in any intelligent way. And, third, they are deeply dismayed and rendered uneasy by your example. You are a horrible warning. In the old days you would have been killed as either useless or a bad luck omen. We are more temperate and we do not kill these days. But we easily tire and we can avoid. So don't press your luck. The others are not fatigued. They are fine and they may just run out of patience.

XII

THE summer waxed. The summer passed. Already half
was gone, thrown away in the hospital. I burned to get up
to the forest, to the summer home at Merriewold that father had left me. I wanted my garden, my woods, my
home around me. But the doctors cautioned against pre-
mature departure. "Stay near us," they said. "Stay near
the laboratory and therapists." I strained and stretched to
get away. And finally, after some weeks of horrid heat,
they said I might. Jonathan came from Cambridge to help
and we loaded up the car and were off.

And then I noticed a very curious thing. I didn't feel it.
I saw it. I became aware only because I couldn't get my
moccasin on. My right foot and leg were swelling past
recognition. Had I broken it? Had I strained it? I told no
one but Pauline. And no one noticed. There was so much
wrong with me that a little thing like a swollen ankle, although it was the size of an elephant's leg, was not to be

considered or even remarked upon. It worried me a good
bit. It didn't pain me, of course. It worried me, because I
thought I should maybe have an X ray taken, maybe in
the local country hospital. I rather dreaded that. I wanted
to stay in the woods, so I kept quiet and worried and
stewed. It turned out to be what the doctors had expected
all along: edema (swelling). It came on at this point only
because I sat still in the car for three long hours with the
leg down. Happily it was no new problem, and their only
remark when they learned was that they were astonished
that I hadn't had it sooner, and more of it, and to quit
worrying.

We got there. I went down my roads again in full
summer. The last time I had seen the parkway leaves
(May, it was), they had scarcely budded. I was lifted out
of the car and put in my chair. And then the beautiful
perfumes of the forest took me in, enfolded me. Pine
scent, pine hot in the sun. Ferns, ferns just beginning
to turn toward autumn, browning. And rhododendron
leaves. I'd missed the whole flowering, of course, but I saw
the dried husks.

Somehow or other they got my chair over the rocks and
into the house. And I was installed in absolute quiet and,
for me, absolute beauty. Walter kept me in the guest cottage, which was ground level and self-contained, consist-
ing of two rooms and a bath—the large room enormous—
the east end entirely glass and opening out on a glade of
ferns traversed at dusk and dawn by wild deer. One could
not see another habitation nor the road. The ceiling of

this huge doll's house was vaulted and walls and ceiling
were of unfinished wood. There were books, nice, sparse
unpainted furniture, two white pallets facing the forest
and enormous mirrors reflecting the forest. Mainly there
was space and quiet except for the sound of branches
brushing the roof, birds, chipmunks and, at night, small
feet scampering overhead. And in this fern-smelling bassi-
net I lay peacefully watching the sun patterns or the
moths around the lamp. I lay snug as a newborn.

Walter brought me every meal from the main house
and the three of us—my husband, my son and I—ate at a
little card table, tranquil in a way we had not been for
twenty-eight years.

The rain took the roof steadily, quietly, forever. It
soaked through the leaves with a pricking sound and it
was lively around the house.

I asked to go to my garden. I was bumped and pushed
over the rocks and grass to the plot, fenced securely
against depredators by chicken wire. I was helped to my
feet and pressed my nose against the mesh. My poor little
garden, forlorn and lost, hardly a trace of it left, a weed
patch.

The grass was heavy with rain. The bushes drooped
and dripped and the great pine branches, glittered and
glistened, bowing to the weather. The air was as spring
and lay like a caress newly on the skin. But it was not
spring. It was mid-August and presaged autumn, and
there was the smell of broken, dead leaves, dank leaves
and rotting wood, a good, acrid, rich smell. This was the

time of chrysanthemums and zinnias, but there were none
in my garden. There were no flowers at all except the
wild asters. My garden was a wilderness, a graveyard of
my former plantings. The flowers could not stand up to
the neglect and the weeds and the devouring deer which
roamed outside and sniffed at them hungrily through the
wire. I looked at it sadly through the wire fence and my
fingers itched to start work, but I could not do anything
and I had to content myself with remembering. I clung to
the wires, wet with raindrops, and looked at the weedy
wastelands, a tangle of briar, blackberry vines, wild bram-
bles; one small phlox, spotted with mildew, pushed its
head through the brush. The garden was gone.

Several times my men brought the chair up through the
rocks from the guest house cottage to the house and en-
gineered my elevation up the porch steps and into my
parlor, my darling parlor with the pink sofas and all the
cozy nooks and crannies, my teasing but dear pictures.
And upstairs? Ah, that was where I could not go! The
stairs of my childhood, the stairs I grew up with, learned
balance on, the escape, the escape from the New York
flat, the stairs that meant freedom, summer. Ah, me! I
gazed at the treads leading into the dark. Up there was
my bedroom, my white bed and the beloved pictures and
the little treasures. Treasures? Gimcrackeries. And the
nursery where I learned to read books . . . Up there beyond seeing. Jonathan's room, with the four-poster and a
crocheted canopy and the beautiful patchwork quilt, the

Texan Lone Star quilt. I couldn't see how my toys did. I couldn't play with them or arrange them. "Is everything . . . ?" "Yes," said Walter, "everything." It would have to wait until next summer.

The dining room with its Canton ware. Walter had not put out the big dishes, nor the museum Meissen. Why go to that trouble? If I were not to be there, why go to that trouble? He'd as lief have eaten on linoleum with paper napkins. In fact, that's what we had for a dinner, served glumly by Pauline, who was getting morbid with the rain.

The dining room is concerned, of course, with food and therefore had been the focal point of my life as a child. It was the place of family interchanges. Seated at the square Edwardian table on ugly manufactured chairs, father had sat at the head, opposite mother, who sat with her back to the syringa bushes and the trees, flanked by Margaret and me, me gabbling without cease, Mag silent, rolling her dazzling, blue, infantile gaze with devastating effect and getting precisely what she wanted, particularly from father; and then in young womanhood, unhappy, mother and I alone, mother trying desperately to be convivial, I silent and surly, miserable with rebellious hate; and then in young marriage, Walter in father's place and I in mother's, I silent—or sort of—with real happiness, and Jonathan growing. All stages of this. Oh, the happy manifold voices that surrounded us! And now I sat in father's place because it was easier to wheel me to, Walter opposite, Jonathan and his love, Rosemary, gentle-voiced, fresh as a rose. I was largely silent because I had lost my voice and found it a tremendous effort to speak or to be heard. It was equally an effort for anyone to listen to me.

"I think," said Jonathan one night in the candlelight, "we would like you to know that we are getting married." I continued to munch stolidly as I always do when moved. They stared at us expectantly.

"Well, aren't you surprised?"

"No. I'm happy and delighted, not surprised."

Walter was busy with champagne.

There had been years when we had thought Jonathan could not live, when we had struggled to keep him barely in existence. (He had been born with a fell congenital disease, Hirschsprung's.) There had been years of terror, in the late sixties, of his going to war, an anxiety augmented by the fact that his birthday was second on Nixon's schedule for draft preference. There had been years when he floundered and groped for what he wanted to do. And now he knew and had a fine job ahead of him and had named his girl and she wanted him. And she was lovely and gifted.

And so we raised our glasses!

Occasionally the sun came out, and when it did I asked to be taken again to my garden, hitherto one jump down from the path and across a stretch of lawn, but now only possible if I took the long way around, slowly and steadily, with my eyes on the uneven turf, such a circuitous route, with no more jumping.

The clover path. I saw ants on the stones and various

beetles and bugs scuttling for safety, who care for nobody and are unselfconscious. I watched an inchworm, the kangaroo of the arthropods, pole-vaulting along the fence. I reached down from my chair on the path, or what had once been a path, and began to weed with my left hand, throwing the discards over my shoulder.

When I was young the open forest glades were happy with flowers, colored butterflies, patches of very green grass. But mainly flowers. And even in my young married days we had a nice garden, festooned and pillared with Dorothy Perkins roses and containing quantities of all good and pleasant old-fashioned blooms. But gradually the woods grew up and the big forest took over, devoured the gardens, obliterated them. The flowers retreated, despite my anxious care, yard by yard, to a very small patch, heavily wired in, patrolled by me. Outside foraged the hordes of red deer, who are voracious and possessed of extremely sharp noses for smelling out succulent leaves and tender new buds. And outside dug the woodchucks, burrowing in, burrowing under, burrowing through to get at my wards. It took a healthy woodchuck about thirty-six minutes to finish off a garden: all of the lilies, all of them, not most of them; delphinium; phlox; lupine; every possible kind of bulb; poppies. Sometimes they left a scarlet, bleeding blossom on the ground. But more often nothing. There was no sign they had been there until one saw the shorn stubble of the stalks and one was aware that suddenly there was no color where there had been a great deal. I hated the woodchucks. I was once so enraged by the depredations of one—who dug in at the far, far corner of the fence and started with the lady's slippers and made his way right down to the front gate, leaving nothing— that I asked the superintendent to set traps, and he did, cruel, killing instruments, cunningly hidden. And the next time I went into my garden to dig, I was aware that there was a live animal close by, panting, and I looked up to see the desperate, beady eyes of a trapped creature. I got Walter and Jonathan, and Jonathan brought his new gun, and then—craven, cowardly creature that I was—I scurried down the road so that I would not witness the execution. Walter said, "Aim for the head." His voice came very clear through the still afternoon woods. And then there was a retort, a single retort, and I went back and the woodchuck was being dragged away to another corner of the garden to be buried and decompose and fertilize the ground he had cannibalized. But I was ashamed of myself and I was ashamed of what I had done to Jonathan. And Walter didn't like it. He doesn't like flowers much, but he didn't like killing. "The most cruel thing was," said Walter, "that he had been caught by the balls." That was not the most cruel thing. The most cruel thing was the dragging away of the lifeless body! All that energy and complexity and appetite stopped in one count! All that astonishing fabrication of life, and in one count the starting of the tremendous cycle of decomposition and elimination! One count.

I have often sat in the garden. I have often felt the sun warm on my face and hands. I have often breathed deep of the morning, but these days I somehow entered into the morning. I *was* the sunlight or the rain. I was the insect life. I was the buzzing and droning and bumping and the silent scrabbling. When a beetle crossed the path, it was as much an event as if a guest had come to lunch. I was neither happy nor unhappy about the bugs. I felt no compassion, neither did I feel kinship. Simply they were alive and I was alive. I observed them crossing the path. That happened. I was aware that that was happening. It was enough. I entered into it and I suddenly realized that I had entered into all the small minutiae of daily living, the sounds in the house, the smells, the happenstance of a voice, footsteps, as though I had been a child again.

I remembered the happy, good days when I had been sick and kept home from school and put to bed in the living room—not in pain, just too sick to go to school—and mother had got out her special books for me to see, her treasures, the Kate Greenaway books, and I had sat with a cup of milk and listened to all the busy sounds of the household, quietly, in the morning—the sounds that were there every day when I was away at school, so pleasant and varied and interesting and not before known to me, not experienced by me except on these extraordinary visitations.

All sounds, particularly voices, were higher then when I was a child, and clearer. They came to the ear fresher, as though they'd never before been heard—the sound of someone hammering, the slamming of a screen door, steps on a wooden floor, wheels, a call—never before heard, an

event in the morning. The mornings held news then.
There was time. Later there would be no time, what with
school, then college, career and marriage, but in early
childhood there was time for the slamming of a door, for
a beloved footfall. And lunch was an achievement and a
climax.

On these occasions when, as a child, I was sick, I didn't
have to do anything at all but lie and look and lie and listen, and to know in my being what was going on. And
now it seemed it was all there for me to know again,
these tiny little events happening daily. And I suddenly
was aware that I was happy, happy in a way that I had
not been before. Happy in the moment, contented, self-
sufficient, trusting. It was enough somehow. I had
stopped sweating after the moment. Great ideas are not
promoted from this nerveless state, nor great art, nor, in
truth, anything at all, except possibly wisdom. I had
reached the condition of the coral polyp and "simply
was" and that was enough.

When I was about eleven or so and my little sister was
eight or nine, Walter Hampden, the actor, produced "The
Light of Asia" at the Theosophical Institute across the
hills from us in Hollywood and played it every night for
an entire summer. It was very beautiful and he was extremely moving. It dealt with the story of the Prince Gautama, who was turned from a life of idleness and self-in-
dulgence by three sights which had been carefully kept
from him by his father: a starving beggar, a leper, and a
rotting corpse. Every night my sister and I listened on our

sleeping porch for the scream when the leper appeared. And then we heard the funeral procession. "Rum, rum, satai, Rum, rum, satai," and the gongs throbbed and the drums beat. Then we went happily to sleep. ("Rum, rum, satai" became part of our secret family language; it meant bad news coming.)

Gautama went off then to sit under the bodhi tree and think about these matters. While he was sitting there he was tempted by various visions: power, riches, beauty, the lust of the flesh. The flesh was personified as his princess bride by Mrs. Walter Hampden, a lady of impeccable morals and milk-toast personality, who read the lines of seduction and compassion like a New Jersey hostess at a tea party. But the dance version of the same character was played by Ruth St. Denis, in a golden sari, sitting behind a pond in which live lotus (and they were live and blooming, I ascertained that) added a final authentic touch to a really beatific vision. And with her gestures and her exquisite manner she begged him to come back to his life with her and told him she was bearing his child.

He resisted. I thought at the time that it was damn hard lines for the young lady. Nobody asked her what she wanted, which was certainly not life on a pot of beans under the bodhi tree. But he was becoming the Buddha and he had to behave so.

And Buddha did some more sitting—a year or two. And while he was still under the bodhi tree, a milkmaid came to draw water at the spring. He asked her how she could endure poverty with nothing but death as a certain end.

And she replied that life was enough for her and she didn't ask to understand; as a seed bears flowers and then fruit, all in season, she trusted that life would unfold and she would be part of the great pattern. And she took joy as she went along in just being there. This was the moment of enlightenment for him.

When he left the bodhi tree and came back to his friends and companions, he was the Buddha and the greatest teacher Asia ever had.

Jonathan read me something from a school book:

Some disciples approached the Gautama-Buddha. "Are you the greatest teacher?" they asked.

"No," he replied, "I am not."

"Are you the most powerful?"

"No."

"Are you the most compassionate?"

"Not even that."

"Are you the wisest?"

"No."

"What are you then?"

And he opened his eyes and, looking at them, said, "I am awake."

Buddhists recognize this, the state of being aware. If the wind is blowing, they're aware of the wind. If they're walking, they're aware of walking. If they are sweeping with a broom, they are aware of the broom and the act of sweeping.

Some of this I had come upon by myself simply because my adult body suddenly became as unmalleable and uncontrollable as that of a lower primate, and the entire function of sleeping or throwing or even walking was to me a complicated and astonishing achievement. I thought of it mechanically, in its difficulties, and I thought of it aesthetically and I thought of it emotionally. I hadn't done this since I was two, but then, of course, I had not really grasped the processes.

All this precludes concentration on any other subject while walking, like writing a book or doing a sum of figures or planning dinner. And, of course, this is what most of us do—or try to do. But I think it is very refreshing and invigorating to call a sharp halt and pay attention. Just simply that. Pay attention to what's going on and what we are doing. I believe we could learn a great deal and we could take joy and power in matters which are usually totally unnoticed.

Delight Walters, my beautiful birthday child, writes me she is now in medical school studying day and night: "I love science with a fascination unending. The mechanism of a single-celled microorganism is incredible and we humans are just too good to be true."

Like a swimmer, I went deeper and deeper into states of being I had never dreamt of before, states of perceiving and feeling that had nothing to do with achievement or business or duty or morals. I was awake.

What I really felt that first summer was that I had died in the hospital. Died dead and now had been reborn and that I was now one year old, and although I looked like an old woman and could barely walk and needed help for every physical thing I did, I yet felt like a little child, young and fresh and full of vigor. And I looked back on my previous life, the entire middle age, as stale, used up, worn out, faded—in short, old—and the new life which had begun since the stroke as a fresh gift. I didn't work at this sensation. I didn't choose it arbitrarily, but I enjoyed it very deeply. I was capable of being forgiven for my faults because I was inexperienced. And I was capable of experiencing all things quite freshly and very colorfully, with new delights and none of the old constraints. And I was capable of growing, of learning new things. It was a feeling of freedom such as I haven't known since I was, in chronological time, five years old.

Mag was an orthodox Christian and believed in the creed and went devoutly to all services. Did she know this peace? "I am the resurrection and the life." "I believe," she said, and that's all she would ever say to me.

And so it was a bridal time for all of us at Merriewold. There in the ferns I had the blessed experience of rediscovering that the man that I had lived with thirty-two years was in love with me. The surprise of this idea lifted me, half-dead and half-finished, out of circumstances and chronology. I was not only a child again. I was ageless.

Not so the woods. They drooped. They dripped. They soaked. It rained almost without cease, and although Walter struggled to keep up his spirits, he got gloomier and gloomier and finally he said he couldn't stand the trip with the food—from the kitchen door through the sopping forest, over the slippery rocks to the rain-battered cottage (I loved the drumming on the roof, I loved the tinkling at the windows, I loved the sight of the mists gathering and dispersing and moving and gathering again under the trees)—and so we must go back to the city and we would lend our house to neighbors.

XIII

NEW YORK—Thanksgiving Day. Jonathan's wedding.
What to wear? How to mask my maimed limbs, my de-
formed feet? Martha Graham called on me robed like an
antique classic queen. I gasped when the door opened.

"Oh, beautiful!" I breathed. "Martha, if I had a gar-
ment like that for my son's wedding!"

"Halston. I'll get him to give you one." She looked at
my feet in moccasins, one twisted and useless, as I sat in
the wheelchair. "And you should wear gold slippers." She
threw me hers. "You have the smallest feet in the business. Gold." Hers were considerably larger and slimmer.
The slippers were made by Capezio.

"Sounds cute."

"Your feet should be cute."

"My feet are twisted."

"Don't ever let on."

Capezio, the dancers' shoemaker, subsequently de-

signed and made for me very pretty slippers of colored
satin to match all my dresses and new Cantonese silk
tunics of rainbow colors. Given the problem, they were
charming. No gold, however.

Halston apparently was unenthusiastic about donating
one of his best models to me, so Martha had delivered her
very own robe, cleaned and pressed and done up in tissue
paper.

The wedding was on Rosemary's birthday, Thanksgiving, and I did not wear gold shoes but ballet slippers,
which proved untrustworthy. (I had arrived at the Essex
House on Central Park South, to the bellboys' dismay, in
broken sneakers and my hair in pigtails. Mary Green su-
pervised the transformation.) I kicked the ballet slippers
off and went in in stocking feet. The ceremony under the
Jewish *chuppah* was no less binding for that.

They looked like all bridal couples: apart, bewitched,
haloed, slightly mussy. They held hands and listened to
the wise and beautiful words.

After the blessing of the bread and the cutting of the
loaf and the toasts, the string trio, which up to then had
played prettily a program of Jonathan's careful choosing,
broke into dance music, and the groom led his bride out
onto the floor. Jonathan had had no dance lessons due to
my great unwillingness to influence him. But he is an
athlete and they had practiced something suitable for
the occasion and somehow he got her very nicely around
the floor. And then, and then . . .

Rosemary went into her father's arms and Jonathan

should have taken me. He took the bride's mother, Sylvia, instead. The full impact of the deprivation, the wretched pattern ahead, hit me right then. Right then at that moment I grasped all the implications.

I wanted to stand up and feel my hands on his shoulders, have him put his hand on my back, lead me. I was a dancer. I wanted to dance him proud. I had to yield my place. Right then I grew old.

I'm ashamed of that moment, but it had to happen sooner or later. Sylvia knew and she was as solicitous of me as though I had been her sister, her wounded sister. Of course, not a word has ever been spoken.

XIV

I HAD given myself twelve months to be on my feet again.

I was stronger now and more durable. Gerry dug in her spurs. Apparently McCagg had given her permission. The therapy sessions were longer and rougher. There was no pity and no excuses were accepted.

Those women intended me to get well whether or no. The treatment was now what I would call professional and, believe me, there was no baby talk.

I went for a therapy class three times a week up to the rehabilitation center on the eighteenth floor of the tower in The New York Hospital. I was always taken out of the cab by the same charming, jolly doorman. He always made the same joke: "On this lovely seat you will delicately place your posterior and enjoy yourself." And I always laughed and we looked at each other affectionately. He was expecting a child and I daresay that he taught him the same joke. But, oh, the kindness and the skill with which he maneuvered me out of the cab and into my wheelchair and back into the cab at the end of my session!

Walk to the end of the barres, then turn, fifteen feet back. And then the chair and rest. But soon I had to walk down the corridor, half step by half step. And then the chair and rest. And try to stop my heart pounding. If I were not so timid, if I were not so frightened. "Is everybody frightened?"

Gerry smiled. "Now, then, try to put all your weight on the right side, on the knee and hand."

"I'll hurt myself. The wrist will buckle."

"Do it. I'm here."

It wouldn't hurt, of course, because in my cement corset I was mummified in unfeeling matter. But there are viscera, moving viscera inside that will be hurt and my breast and my chin and my teeth and the wrist.

"Try."

The next day back on the mat and a charming man beside me, a new one. He looked over at me gently when his therapist had turned away. He smiled. "I can't do it either. Don't be ashamed."

"I'm so frightened."

"We're all frightened."

The clientele was fairly mixed. The damaged, the mutilated, the imbecilic, the wounded and all combinations thereof. There was, for instance, a middle-aged black, a strapping fellow who had just lost his leg at the hip. I'm told it was diabetes. He spent all his time pulling on weights and strengthening his arms so that he would be able to manage crutches and the prosthesis. He wouldn't smile and he wouldn't speak and he wouldn't reply to, "Good morning." He just quietly and persistently pulled. And there was an eighty-year-old woman, very fragile, who had just lost her leg at the hip and was practicing pushing on her poor arms so that she could manage crutches. And there was a small eight-year-old Brazilian boy who had fallen down a flight of stairs and had never been quite in order since. When I say quite in order I mean he couldn't walk. They practiced with him on the double barres, and when he found that he could race up and down he did race up and down without stop, yelling.

One day they tried a new brace on him. It was uncomfortable and strange. He screamed and wailed without stop at the top of his lungs and then he found that he liked it, liked it very much, and that reaction was not any quieter. He discovered the weights. He discovered the pulleys. He discovered the mechanical bicycle and the scales. I think that Edward, the therapist, finally had to take him off under his arm, down the corridor, and he went off hollering, his legs and arms waving like a distraught spider while the rest of us inert hunks lay on our pallets thinking of going back to quiet rooms, thinking of having cups of tea, thinking of pillows and TV.

There was a delightful elderly man. He'd been a professor of history and his son brought him to the room. Like me he was an outpatient. He could no longer speak, but his son understood his mewing and gabbling and was able to do what he wanted and help him into his boots and out of them. And he came twice a week faithfully and mewed at us. He'd been the head of his department.

And there was a beautiful young girl of about twenty-two who seemed quite sound and whole. "What is the matter with her?" I asked. Gerry rolled her eyes. "We simply don't know. We think nothing. We cannot get her to leave the gymnasium or to leave treatment. She takes up our time and she takes up our attention and there is nothing wrong with her, but her father pays and so what can we do?"

Down to the end of the barres and back. Watch in the mirror. Watch how the right leg throws out. Watch how the right foot twists spastically. Watch how the hips jerk out of balance. It's time for you to stop this. Now put both hands on the barre. Pick up the right foot. Put it back and cross the left leg under. Now over.

"You mean a pas de bourrée?"

"Whatever you call it. Do it."

"Oh, Gerry, you should have see my pas de bourrée on point. It was like silk."

Day after day. Nobody talked in this room. No "very good!" And a terrible effort. Not to the point of sweat but to the point of shudders and panting.

I grew very attached to the women therapists and to Edward, my slouched Viking, and when one of them left to take another job or, in one case, to go to South America with a patient, we all mourned her departure although we all wished her well. Several of the therapists had become ballet fans and I used to hold short seminars on the edge of my mat with a ring of them gathered around me.

They had seen Baryshnikov, and can you imagine what that godlike movement meant to women who dealt all day with the crippled, the maimed, and the partial?

And then one day there was my handsome one-legged black in a business suit, looking very spruce and very distinguished and walking on two legs, a little stiffly but with no trace of a limp.

"Good Lord," I said, "you're a handsome man!" And then he smiled for the first time. "You look absolutely smashing!" And he smiled some more. I was, of course, at the moment practicing crawling on all fours on a practice mat. I did not look distinguished and I did not look smashing.

We attempted stairs, a short flight of steps with rails on each side.

I attempted to walk down the hall briskly in my ballet slippers with my tripod cane. I went for about ten feet and then suddenly . . . whoops! Edward, who was passing, saved me by a sudden lunge. The foot had gone with the ankle, my entire weight plunging. The little therapist who had me (not Gerry this time) was scared to the teeth. She had to sit down. "You shouldn't do that," she said.

"No," I said. "Of course not," and sat down opposite her. We panted at each other.

Suddenly one day I was aware that I felt weight on my right side. I knew when the foot was on the ground. I knew when I had put weight on the foot. This was an enormous breakthrough.

XV

IT WAS now more than six months since the initial insult and Dr. Plum said I must come in for an examination, a very quiet, searching, painstaking test. He said finally, "I think you're getting a little feeling back, but not much."

And I asked him point-blank, "Is this the way it's going to be? Is this what I live with?"

And he said, "I think so. I believe so. You will have to learn to cope with this."

"For life?"

"I'm afraid so."

A death sentence.

I didn't even blink. My right arm, my right leg, that whole side of my body gone. I was to be two bodies, one of them not my friend, alien. And must I drag this creature about with me, this Siamese horror, forever? Forever not my friend? Very likely. From now on my body was to live in two different tempi, the left side, which was nor-

mal and healthy and was, I believe, young for its age, and
the right, which was not only very old but broken. The
left brisk, the right lethargic. Of course, the right would
drag down the left.

I didn't quail at the idea because I simply refused to
consider it. This is my way of dealing with unpleasant
matters. Except death, of course. That cannot be over-
looked. And deep down I had the sense that this, this
nothing at all, also was final.

Dr. McCagg said, "No, not necessarily so." But I knew.

Plum is one of the great neurologists of the world and
his word is taken by hospitals, governments, rulers. His
word is law in many places. He is, among other things,
the greatest living expert on coma. (That had nothing to
do with me at the moment. That was something for me to
look forward to.) He knew well what he was talking
about and he said I would never feel normally again on
my right side and my leg and my hand would never feel
again and never move normally.

Fred Plum later said, "Your body didn't get better. You
did."

At Christmastime I went down to the fourteenth floor
at the hospital, which had been my old habitat, and
brought the nurses at the floor desk boxes of cakes and
candies. Some of them remembered me. There I encoun-
tered Dr. Patterson, the surgeon who had cut out my
carotid artery. I reminded him that he had promised that
in two months I'd barely remember that I'd ever had a

stroke. I was walking with the tripod, very slowly and haltingly. "Look, Doctor," I said, "the state I'm in."

He took in the situation and then remarked rather casually and amusedly, "Well, that just proves what a liar I am, doesn't it?" And he smiled pleasantly and went about his business.

I was told I would have an audition, an audition of walking, before the entire medical staff of the rehabilitation center. I had always walked with beauty, even, on occasion, with nobility, and when I crossed the stage it was memorable. I knew what a human walk could be, so I tried this time with as much gallantry and debonaire verve as I could muster with my tripod, and my foot only turned over once. I wore moccasins. I found that my foot did not turn in moccasins and sneakers, whereas if I put on a hard sole, no matter how low the heel, the ankle went right over and I never knew and I plunged. So this time I walked up and down the trial room and the head doctor said to me, "I think you need a brace." And they brought me a brace to examine—two chromium bars with a leather strap to go around the leg below the knee—and my pretty, pretty leg and my beautiful ankle were to be in a cage. I was a cripple. I turned my eyes away and went ashen. I didn't expect to be wholly well ever again, but viable certainly. A brace. A cage. A contraption. Like a polio victim. Like the March of Dimes.

McCagg explained quietly that I would feel confident,

that my muscles would strengthen while I was learning confidence.

"They will be weak," I said. "I must not have a crutch."

"No," she said, "they will be stronger. You will do exercises to make them stronger and you will have confidence." So they gave me a prescription and sent me up to West 116th Street, and there I was measured and fitted and I had to go back five different times and it took five weeks to complete the brace fastened to a pair of boots. But McCagg was right: When I stumped about the first time in my brace I was astonished at the support and comfort. The doctors at The New York Hospital were afraid to put me in any other kind of brace because of the difficulty and danger in fitting unfeeling flesh. But then Dr. Sarno, of the Rusk Institute, looked at the heavy braces, double bars clamped onto my foot and attached to a leather cuff beneath the knee. "Medieval," he said in disgust, and he made me a brace modeled on a plaster cast of my leg, a spiral brace of plastic that screwed on and could be put on and off with one hand. It weighed only eight ounces and fitted into any shoe, a miracle of design. This gave me enormous freedom. I did not have to be helped to get in and out of my boot and I could wear pretty shoes safely. I was safe in bare feet and safe in sneakers, but, as friends rather tartly pointed out, bare feet and sneakers were not appropriate for me to wear to dinner parties.

I began to wear Chinese trousers. I have always de-

spised the vogue for trousers, considering them bad design for the female body as well as gross and self-indul-
gent. But in the countries where women wear trousers,
they also wear long coats or tunics, and they never expose
their bottoms, which after age thirty are usually unattractive. So I bought Chinese suits with long coats and the
brace was hidden in my pants and I was told I looked
very smart. The alternate was my pretty dresses with the
short skirts and the exposure of my entrapped leg and
the heavy surgical boot.

My closet now took on the colors of a paint box. Chinese silks, Indian silks. I had always been discreet about
color, being a redhead and unable to wear pinks or
mauves or reds—or so I thought. Now I was white-headed
and I could wear anything I liked, and I liked brilliant
colors. I threw away the blacks and the grays and the
browns of middle age and went hog-wild, indulging myself with the loveliest tunics and Indian Benares silk pants
of contrasting or complementary tones and little colored
slippers. The more decrepit my body, the more dashing
my dress—plain but très gai, très daring. Another flag
went up the mast to signal my recovering and making my
new life a happy one.

I already owned a closet full of shoes, some very beautiful, custom-made in Florence by Ferragamo. I kept the
most beautiful ones as a sign that I must strengthen my
foot so that I could wear them again. And the precious
ones I put away in tissue paper and hoarded, but there
were sacks of the others. I gave most of them to Judy Ep-

stein, the tiny dancer, because she was the only one with
small enough feet to wear them. It was a wrench, but I
thought somebody had better make use of them. About
the gala slippers I was more selfish and I was much more
superstitious. If I gave these up it would be like abandon-
ing my foot, chopping it off at the ankle.

Not that I was self-conscious about being a cripple. It
was obvious that I was, and there was no use pretending
that I wasn't. I was a cripple in the street and I was a
cripple in the home. But I always felt that it was an impo-
sition on other people's sensibilities to force the ugly accoutrements on their attention when it wasn't necessary.

But, on the other hand, I was not self-conscious about
going around in the chair in the street; I had to, so I
went. On Saturdays and Sundays Walter used to take me
for delicious strolls through Greenwich Village and south
of Washington Square, and we visited the Italian district
and went to the cappuccino shops and had coffee and
whipped cream together, and he used to park the chair
and negotiate the grotesque, crablike entrance into shel-
ter and get me seated on one buttock (like the nurse in
Candide) and feed me very beautifully and then wheel
me home. I indulged myself in the wheelchair for some
months and then I sent it away and went it alone. This
was hard but necessary. It demanded a great deal of both
Pauline and me. Now I had to walk from the taxi up to
the elevators, a long walk in The New York Hospital, and
I used to measure off the distance on the marked linoleum
floor. My gaze was, of course, down at my feet, where it

had to be. Fortunately doctors look where they're going and never bumped into me. Not bumping is part of their calling. Later, when I attempted to go to the theater, I had to give more than attention and, most important, I could not pay attention to the curiosity I aroused. But I was so intent on getting back into life that I really didn't give a damn. People seemed not to stare unduly. Or did they? I suppose they did behind my back, and maybe they whispered, but I didn't care. I was saved from shame by my all-engrossing interest and also by my curiosity. I let other people pick up the pieces, and the other people generally were Walter and the pieces were quite often me, and I think he was frequently humiliated. He has always been handsome and well dressed and effective in his appearance. Now he was the companion of a freak and the service he rendered had no end in sight. It presupposed a very real modicum of unselfish courage.

I remember our first trip together to an evening theater performance. We went early in order to avoid the crowd and, of course, were sitting ducks for attention and renewed acquaintance. And then we left before the end of the last act in order to avoid the crowd at the close and get a cab, and I had to stumble up the aisle, which was sharply raked and which was acutely difficult for me, carrying my fur coat and my purse. Carrying my fur coat and purse with what? I dropped them. Walter couldn't put me down in order to pick up the fur coat and a stranger had to help. There was I, who had been one of the best-known figures in the American theater, stumbling, creeping, half crawling. Walter considered it beyond expression, not exactly shameful but dreadful, like a figure hanging on a gibbet. We got out and we got home. Walter needed a drink.

But he went again. And again and again. And we saw quite a few plays, although Walter found the experience wearing. I experienced nothing except extreme exasperation. It is my belief that if the subject really feels no embarrassment or shame, there is none.

This story is an attempt to tell the candid truth as I remember it, and so I am constrained to admit this fact: I have always liked being the center of attention and I have very frequently achieved this. Now I was a freak, but I was still the center. See? I truly believe that if I had been beautiful I would have been insupportable the whole of my life.

Once Walter hired a limousine to fetch us at the opera, and because of traffic I had to rush and take the backseat. I was in full evening dress, and when it came time to get me out I lay on the floor of the cab and he and the chauffeur hauled me out prone by the feet.

Due to my profound respect—even affection—for living performers, I had never once walked out on an unfinished play while there were actors on the stage, no matter how obnoxious, no matter how tedious, not once, although I cursed them or blasted them afterward verbally. But now I found I had to. If Walter and I waited to the end in decent decorum, we had to go out with the mob, and the crowd commandeered the taxis. There were none for us ever, and Walter could not leave me standing while he went foraging. There are never any seats in New York theater lobbies. There was no place to wait. We have sometimes been searching for a taxi for as long as half an hour, with me clinging either to a trash basket or a lamp-post. We now leave early or, in some lucky instances, if the theater is close to a good restaurant, we walk to the restaurant, have a drink and then get a cab, which the doorman politely fetches. I hereby make my apologies to all the actors and dancers I have affronted. I was driven by necessity.

I could not get out of a tub of water without help. And for the same reason I could not sit in the rear of a taxi because I could not push forward and push myself upright. I had to sit always in the front seat, in which I just slid into place. All drivers accepted me in front, although it's against the law, except the Checker cabs. They won't. And Chinese drivers. They won't. The rest do gladly, and on the whole they have been wonderfully kind and help-ful. I tipped well and the drivers were pleasant. Once in a while they were interested and I could always tell their nationality by their identification cards, and the for-eigners were kindest. I have only met two or three men who have refused to help me out of the cab and only two others, both young, who were rude and tried to extort money.

I made several attempts at going in taxis alone. Well, I could very nicely if someone put me into a taxi and if the driver helped me out. That was simple. But I had to have a taxi to get into and I learned one very interesting fact: Taxis will not stop for a lone cripple. If I were with somebody they would stop, but not for me singly. Will not.

In this kind of catastrophe it is not only the individual who suffers the stroke. The family is involved and must rise to form a bastion of support. The service demanded is stringent and sacrificial. And it is more: It is unremitting; it is for life. Not enough attention has been paid to families. They deserve, I believe, the lion's share of the credit for salvaging, and they generally get very little. The spouse's role is exacting, harder than the victim's because of the curtailments which are galling without the anesthesia of weakness, of self-interest, self-concern, attention and praise. The patient, let us say, approximately cuts his meat and everyone cheers and bends a beaming eye, but who regards the husband or wife waiting quietly for the slow pushing of food around the plate, the wavering passage to the mouth, the lengthy mastication, the waiting while dinner is long over, waiting every night, every dinnertime, and then cleaning up the slops and spills? And all merrily and humorously and with grace. This is more than is demanded of mothers who bank on hope.

Walter, have I thanked you?

At first, after the stroke, I had been apologetic for not bringing him morning coffee, lying in bed luxuriously instead. Gradually I took it for granted. Gradually I just let him do for me. Expected him to. Demanded him to. Was it galling for him? He never let on.

"It's been the making of me."

And then our son: For this reason and that, including illness, he'd had a tormented childhood, a difficult youth and early manhood. For a long time he was edgy, nervous, ill at ease with us and we with him. It was hard to talk. It was hard to be together. He was almost totally uncommunicative. And the family had felt split up, which was agony for all of us. But suddenly we were not separated, and now there he was, a mature man, wise, helpful, with bonny grace and wit, not his father's but his own. Now he spoke to us freely and easily, with absolute tranquillity and love.

And my sister, ah, sweet Mag! Over the years we'd grown so far apart, both desperately ambitious, fighting for the last word, the most noticed, the most successful (in her case), the most interesting (in mine), self-supporters! We had not been friends for years and here we were, sisters again, as we had been when schoolgirls, relishing the jokes, gossiping, taking pride in each other's small triumphs. At peace. Why? I was a broken husk and Mag was contaminated, but we were at peace and in love because we trusted.

After the stroke everyone bent entire efforts to understanding me, but now I found, quite simply, that I could understand others. What's more, I wanted to. I trusted without fear of being hurt. All my defenses were smashed and there they were, the others. I had a sister again. I had a son. I had, ah wonder, a love. I could not have had this new perception without the breaking. I had not been wise enough to choose. It happened like leaves growing.

It was inward, not always apparent. But it was there.

"I'm gentler now," I said.

"You're what!" gasped Lucia, Oliver, Jim, Gemze, Tom, Dick, Harry, and Svetlana. "That'll be the day!"

But they didn't know. No matter that, due to habit, I still snapped. It was a way of speaking. My heart had gone out of it. I was gentle because I had grown trusting.

My husband loved me, and I could now love him so that he could bear it. That was the point of the whole exercise.

I once knew a wonderful old lady in Philadelphia. Social Register, Old Family, Pillar of Society, the works. She married when middle-aged, a dashing doctor ten years her junior, only to discover after decades of happiness—when, in fact, she was eighty—that he had taken a paramour. Her anguish was horrible. Then, one twilight as she was sorting laundry, she suddenly realized what she must do to serve him: She must love him the very best she could. Simply that, no more. The clarity and simplicity of this revelation was so startling that she fainted away and was found unconscious among the linen.

She told me this two days later. A week after, she died. So great is the power of revelation.

My semibeatitude lasted. All my senses were distorted and magnified. I later told a priest, Father Harkey. He said he understood. I think priests do understand about this. Probably all religious people do. But I was not a religious believer. I had reached it by drifting, but I had had to forfeit my body for it. That had been the price which I did not choose to pay but which had been exacted. And that was part of being alive, too.

Spring was here again. I asked to go back to Merriewold and we invited Margaret. She had always come to us for a visit in Merriewold. She had regained her strength and went regularly to the golf course and pursued all her activities—civic, domestic and political. Just one week out of eight had to be given up to poison, and that, of course, was cruelly hard, but she was stalwart and she had learned how to endure it. In the spring she organized a lecture for me in her town down in Easton, Maryland, housed me, cared for me, and gave me a gala afterward. She was such a prodigy of recovery that her doctor asked her to visit other terrified, depressed patients and show off before medical meetings. She became a known case; someone who had really licked cancer. When in New York she asked me out to lunch or dinner and she asked me to her friends' houses to visit her—difficult but fun. I leaned on her arm, of course, wherever I went and she supported me, and there we were, the de Mille girls, Ag and Mag, the scourge of the community, one with a fatal disease and one a cripple, tottering about and being amiable and making each other laugh. Her progress in recovering seemed swifter than mine because I was beginning to realize that my condition would not alter and that for the rest of my life what I had to do was to train an uncouth lump.

But Margaret walked triumphant. She had done it! She had beaten the dreaded horror. Other people succumbed. She did not. But in truth Margaret was frail. She lost a fearful amount of weight. She now was under a hundred pounds, but she wore marvelously becoming clothes and did not expose the bones or scrawny muscles. She was growing bald. She *was* bald, she told me, although I never saw her. She wore a wig and looked attractive and absolutely natural. It was, of course, a good wig. Margaret saw to that. And her mind was diamond-hard and diamond-clear and she remarked on everything that happened around her.

Above all, she was no longer terrified.

She had accepted her age and her condition. I had to learn to accept mine.

In our Hollywood garden in my youth there was a sundial, and around the bronze numerals was a legend, a line from Browning:

> Grow old along with me!
> The best is yet to be . . .

It was nonsense, I always thought as a child, a rigamarole an aging person thought up to make himself feel better. The old were really no use and undoubtedly they felt very badly about that. And who cared?

Well, I'm not sure even now that anyone cares, but I do

know that the poetry is wise and that Browning knew
what he was talking about. Old age is an odd state, a condition of continual diminishing. Activities are curbed.
Physical perceptions are lessened. Friends die, one by
one. But so, thank God, do enemies. And if one's beloveds
fall away, person by person, there is young growth which
we may not be acquainted with, of course, but which we
can observe and which is not necessarily hostile. And although the senses dim and the debilities hasten with attendant small catastrophes, as in a crumbling building—a
cornice, a brick here, a floor there, and then, incon-
veniently, the whole facade—still there are other qualities
that last. There were such a lot of irritations and teasings
and vexations and torturings when young that one is now
excused. In plain words, one doesn't care so intensely, and
whether this is good or bad I cannot say. Certainly it does
not engender intense activity and it would not do for very
young people to know this tranquillity. But the older ones
are permitted to experience it and ought to.

It would be nice if old bodies gained in value the way
old porcelain does, but porcelain remains unchanging and
bodies, alas, alter. And while the colors and textures of
decay are, in themselves, quite beautiful, their connota-
tions dismay us and we recoil toward health and youth.
And this is a very good thing, because if we preferred
what was old and decrepit, where would we soon be?
"Old age is strong stuff," a doctor once said. To him "old
age is not for sissies."

Self-love and pride are so closely linked to the body

that when this goes we feel all is lost. So we say when we are young—and rightly, I believe—but when we are old there is another scale of judging and feeling and it is not just compensatory. It is different. I scorn the smug, spiritual self-congratulation of the deprived. No, this is a genuine shifting of needs and wants as basic as depth pressure to a fish. We need other things and, wonderfully, they are there for us to have.

All the aforesaid is totally invalidated if there is pain. Then the story is different and one can only set one's teeth and pray.

Whenever I felt smug I heard that voice in the hospital: "Don't hit me! Don't do it again! Oh, please, not again!"

What do you do with your time? Oh, nothing much, this and that, a little bit of writing, soon maybe some supervising of my dances, now and then maybe plotting a new dance. Nothing much. The time goes. What did a sailor do when he was at sea? Nothing much. He kept alive. He made the ship go. And there was the sea, of course. Lots to think about there. Nothing much.

XVI

By now a year and a quarter had passed in apparent idleness and I longed to do something—anything—to show that I was alive and could still work, that I had some value. Tranquillity was one thing, inertia another.

While I had still been in the hospital I had received two invitations for shows, one from Arnold Saint-Subber, the producer of *Kiss Me, Kate,* for a new Alan J. Lerner and Leonard Bernstein show on life in the White House called *1600 Pennsylvania Avenue,* and the other for *Rex,* the new Richard Rodgers show about Henry the Eighth. I said I was interested, believing that I would be able to handle a professional job by that first October. I read the Lerner script and didn't like it. But I did like the Rodgers script. In October, however, I learned quite by chance that my one-time assistant, Dania Krupska, had been hired in my place for the job and without a word to me. The producer hemmed and hawed but explained that he felt that I wasn't up to the job physically. I flew into a passion at this, a real old-time Aggie rage! (So much for tranquillity! My newfound wisdom! Bah!) So there it was, two big shows taken from me on the grounds of health and I could see quite plainly that that was the way that it was going to be. Nobody would trust me now with responsibility no matter how gallantly they offered me an arm across the room. This was a fact, however bitter, and it was going to be my fact for life. It was like being young and knowing that I was going to grow up to be ugly.

I did not bow to this decision gracefully. There had been a time in the forties when I had first refusal of every good show that was mounted in New York City, and later I shared this position only with Jerome Robbins. But at first for three years I was the Number One box office attraction.

For the last twelve years or so, however, long before my stroke, I had been tortured by a feeling of extreme disappointment, extreme malaise. The plain truth was—and I faced it nightly and daily all day—that I knew I had not done what I wished to do, what I was capable of. I was wasted. I was squandering my own time.

I wanted to compose good dances, really beautiful, lasting dances, and the dances I had done had been sprightly, adroit, timely, diverting but peripheral, unrooted. I believed, nevertheless, I could do good ones, had even approached them now and then, the dances that suggest more than is visible on the stage. Only now and then had I been able to achieve this. I had spoken to Jerry

Robbins about how quickly the good ones came, the dances that were composed in an hour, not more, and at the first trial, from start to finish, the dances that seemed easy, easy to do and easy to watch and were inexplicably good, without days and days of preliminary work, without rejections and disappointments and despairing. Those were the dances composed instinctively, whole. Suddenly they were there, as if one had peeled back from the very nerve of the heart all the flesh and all the confusion, and had let the essence in, revealed the core simply and truthfully. And Jerry agreed. But they were rare. And for me these opportunities were growing fewer and fewer. These dances had not always been preserved in ballets. Some of them had occurred in commercial shows and were lost, although I had tried frantically to save them. Nobody seemed to have cared but me. And now came the realization that I could not go on working and that the dances would all be lost and that I was, in effect, a failure.

Walter didn't seem to understand.

"You're famous," he said. "You aren't as great as some, but you are famous and," he added a little wistfully, "you have had such success as I never dreamt of." Well, I had worked for it. I had hungered for it and striven for it. I had wanted it. Why I had wanted it is another matter, but I did and I was being denied it and I was bitter and frightened.

Walter had said, "This is not the essence of life. What has this got to do with your being alive and savoring and enjoying life?" I expect other people, certainly artists, will understand. Jerry, of course, did, since he was tortured and dogged by a similar need to go on composing better and better dances. The absolute necessity, like that which drives a prisoner struggling for air. He had to continue struggling, as did I. And I think Walter did too, although he found it dangerous to encourage me.

For so long I had found myself in the gray land surrounded by growing age and there was seemingly no exit from the terrain. Now my senses and my agony were only anesthetized while I waited. But I had not died, I had not ceased. I felt that something must happen, something must give way, but there was no sign and it was not to be, of course, necessarily so. Indeed, the bewilderment, the numbness might intensify. Plainly I would never do what I had intended to do; I would die unachieved. Well, what had I intended to do? What did I really want? If I had known what I wanted, why didn't I do it? If I really had known. I *wanted* to be great. Why? I didn't think I was vain, I didn't really believe that I was egotistical. I had, for instance, never wanted to be beautiful, mainly because I couldn't be and knew it and accepted the fact. But I believed that I could be great if I wanted to hard enough. That, of course, had been nonsense. I could be other things. My burning desire was indeed an act of fantasy, a mark of raw egotism. Why did I want to be great? Because it was ME. All my youth, all my maturity I had burned, had immolated myself with my own hungers and, as a result, what I was able to bring to my art was ashes, and they were ashes of vanity. There are such things as

Igor Moiseyev and his daughter. Margaret looks radiant.

And it was that night that she perceived that she was gathering the poisonous liquid again and that the disease had returned and was progressing full steam ahead.

The next day she phoned me to thank me for the party and to tell me her fearful news. Oh God! There seemed to be no escape from this entrapment, this filthy involvement. And she had thought she had. She had really believed she had.

When I was slowly, slowly making my way from one tiny achievement to another, creeping, stumbling, collapsing, my sister was fighting against cancer and the bimonthly bouts of poisoning which racked her, laid her flat and terrified her.

One night after the Handel Medallion celebration she went back from my triumphs to an empty house in Maryland and began living alone for what was left of her time. She had a daughter, though not in the same town, and she had loving and devoted friends who were in daily attendance and solicitous with favors and food and flowers. But the nights were hers to be endured alone, with all their attendant dismays and regrets and bewilderments and emptiness. Each evening she had her dinner, which she made herself, on a little tray, and she had the TV. And she had her weakness and her regular nausea. And she had terror. Nobody to talk to, nobody's hand to touch, nobody to call out to. I thought she should have a friend with her, a companion, someone. She thought not. "No need," she said, "absolutely no need." And she lived

knacks and skills and there is such a thing as great talent. One doesn't have it just by wanting. One has it or one does not have it. But what is very true, what is enduringly true, is that one has something that is essentially wonderful and this is most certainly life. But one must really know what one has, one must really experience it, serve it.

I read recently that Boris Pasternak had trained as a painter and was a good one, like his father, but then decided it was too difficult for him and that he did not truly want to become a painter if it were to prove that hard. Whatever he chose to be, he sensed, would have to be more felicitous, more instinctively right and natural. The difference, however, between following an instinct surely and indulging laziness can become confused; not, however, in a vigorous spirit.

Don't think that all this was assimilated and absorbed or even perceived within a week, or a month, or a year. But in a few years, gradually, steadily I came to understand all this and accept it and realize that my life had changed. It was not a quick process because it was not superficial. A lifetime's habits of feeling had to be dropped; that isn't quite as difficult as habits of talking or moving, but it is difficult. In this case it dealt with the very roots of personality, but it made for happiness and, above all, it made for peace. I think it was what is called wisdom. A very slow process. It began that first summer in the garden.

So now, now what? Let it go. That part of my life had phased right out. I could perhaps have made a comeback.

For what? Did I really want the intensive hurly-burly and frenzy of the Broadway competition? Did I really want to go on with that now and to the end of my life? It occurred to me, not immediately but slowly and gently, that I did not want anything of the sort, that I really did not care. That was done with. I must find other ways to live and work.

I really did not care.

And then this door opened.

At this very point Lucia Chase and Oliver Smith of American Ballet Theatre offered to give me a gala, with an entire evening of my works, at the New York State Theater at Lincoln Center in New York. In rehearsals I got to work. And suddenly I was not tired. Here was health and rebirth. The dancers of the company were attentive, quiet, docile and solicitous. I had never seen a more mannerly company in my life.

When, however, dress rehearsal came around, we ran into the usual chaos. But this time we were in an enormous theater and I was unable to get up on the stage and had to stay in the audience and communicate through a loudspeaker across a distance of three or four hundred yards, unable to indicate by hand or foot exactly what I wanted. The stagehands, lights, music, scenery and attendant hubbub were wearing.

"Quiet down," said Pauline, bringing me some coffee. "Don't get excited."

Don't get . . . ? Oh, yes, indeed!

The dancers became confused and at one point the en-

tire cast tried to exit through a single small aperture an jammed up helplessly. I shrieked for them to try agai but they still didn't understand, and since my assistant Bill Carter and Vernon Lusby, both absented themselve at that moment for some reason, I was constrained t howl, literally howl, "Will nobody help a cripple?"

This brought heads from every corner of the stage, from the wings, from the pit, from the side aisles. Nora Kaye dropped what she was doing, which was casting for The Turning Point, and came out with great concern. And Scott Douglas raced down to lend aid. And I said, "Scott, you don't know this ballet."

He said, "I know dancing. I can help you."

I said, "Someone go up and show those fools how to get off stage."

Everybody turned to me and said, "You mustn't do this. You will be ill."

Will nobody help a cripple?

Walter laughed until he was sick when he heard the story. The sheer blackmail of it!

The evening was fine. At intermission Abraham Beame, the mayor of New York, handed me, in front of the audience, the Handel Medallion, reading the citation, which ended with the phrase that brought tears to my eyes: "Good citizen."

Afterward DeWitt Hanes of Winston-Salem, North Carolina, gave me a superb party at Le Poulailler. I have a picture taken there of my beautiful sister dining with

through the hours, the long, lasting terrible hours between two and six in the morning, realizing that the new
day brought no surcease, no change, no betterment, but a
greater weakness and a stronger certainty that this was
termination. And not once in all the time that was left,
not one single time did she say to me, "I'm frightened" or
"I'm depressed"; not once did her voice break or quiver;
not once did she lay on me any part of her anguish.

I thought about her always. My ebullience, my good
cheer was weighted with her dark certainty. She knew
this and she knew that I, too, was fighting. She was gallant. She never made the slightest demand. She used to
call around six in the afternoon when my nap was over
and before Walter got back from the office. We talked
family news, gossip, political chitchat. It was our voices
that counted, the sound of our voices. She wanted to hear
my voice at dusk, which is a very bad time. The early evening hours can be cruel.

XVII

WHENEVER there was an hour and I felt strong enough or
clearheaded enough, I worked on my book. I wrote a paragraph here, a paragraph there, and fitted them together
like a jigsaw puzzle. I fitted them very patiently with the
fingers of my left hand and my right paddle and claw. I
couldn't clip pages together. I couldn't find pages that
were missing. I couldn't retrieve pieces of paper that fell
to the ground. But I wrote in longhand and I dictated in
my very thick, low speech into a tape recorder, and Mary
transcribed all faithfully and we fitted them into what
had once been a script of quite another book. Kate Medina, my editor at Doubleday, had said that she would
buy the book, and when I was strong enough, sometime
in the summer, she gave me a lunch in the Doubleday
suite to confirm the sale and there were editors and pub-
licists present. And this, of course, heartened me enormously and I went back and fitted some more. Pretty

Kate had said that Doubleday would publish, so I must hasten. Pasting the manuscript together, pre-stroke and post-stroke, meant overwhelming fatigue and frustration, but delight, too. Kate came to work with me. Hours and hours we sat at adjoining card tables and I scrabbled around in the compost heap I called my manuscript and clawed out this piece and that piece, and we studied the matter. She picked up what I dropped. She fetched what I could not reach, but she never once, not in all those long hours, reached out and said, "Give me the scissors. I'll cut," or "I'll paste," or "I'll write this." She waited while I laboriously and so very badly got through the chore, although her impatience must have risen to the nostrils. She never looked at her watch and said, "I have not enough time for this." She made time. It was astonishing for a senior editor at a big firm and showed a greatness of spirit and understanding that I have seldom met.

And she was heartening. My corrections were, of course, very slow and I saw my way through the disjointed scraps of reminiscences and the wispy bits of narrative imperfectly, taking weeks to find any definite points of concentration. But throughout she said, "You will and it will be good." Her confidence was like a guideline in a cave, a rope around my waist as I toiled on the ascent back to health. I suppose she knew this. She must have.

Doctors ask me so often, "What shall I tell my patients?" And all I can say is, "The patient must have a project, something definite to do, to work toward." I had the book and Kate said it was publishable and I didn't believe it was entirely charity on her part, so I struggled. Among other things, it provided me with the most astonishing hand therapy. I learned to put paper clips back on paper, to sort papers, to stack them evenly, to lift them without spilling, to hunt through piles of them to find the one that I wanted. Someday, just as a lark, tie your best, or active, hand behind you and try with the other, alone, unaided, to do these things.

I continued through the ensuing months, plodding slowly at the job, dictating into little cassettes which Mary transcribed in widely spaced lines so that I could make corrections between, and writing out the more intricate passages in script I couldn't read back but which somehow she alone in the world deciphered. If I wished to see another chapter, I had to send Pauline into my workroom and explain to her what it looked like and ask her to bring it to me. I kept them in separate compartments of the Japanese *tansu* my father had used to store his shirts in and in a music cabinet of long, very shallow drawers. And I had to remember which chapter was in which drawer (don't think they were consecutive; they were not). I went over the manuscript so often that we were all quite bewildered. I used to say, "I don't rewrite this manuscript, I practice it." But it did begin to sound like English prose, and that made me very happy. Pauline was exhausted.

XVIII

I RECEIVED various invitations that tantalized me: from
Imelda Marcos, the first lady of the Philippines, an all-ex-
penses-paid trip ("Are you crazy?" gasped my doctor,
George Gorham. "Fifteen hours over the Pacific! I think
not."); from the Banff Festival of the Arts, permitted and
enchanting; from Ottawa for the Royal Winnipeg Ballet's gala production of *Rodeo;* and to have dinner with
the king and queen of the Belgians, and Pierre Trudeau,
permitted and unforgettable; and then, in October 1976,
from President Gerald Ford to attend the ceremonies
when Martha Graham received the Medal of Freedom—
the first dancing girl ever to be granted such an honor,
the first dancing girl to stand up beside generals and he-
roic soldiers and very great statesmen and learned scientists. The entire profession lifted its head and stood on
tiptoe. And Martha had seen to it that I got an invitation.

Walter could not go and so I asked the columnist Byron

Belt, of the Long Island newspaper *Newsday*, to escort me, and I went off with Pauline and Byron to Washington with my best dress and high hopes for the evening.

The hotels were bulging with theatrical people, the most ornate and famous of the theater and motion-picture world. We got tricked out in our bonnyest clothes and went off together to the White House. We were ushered in and then I discovered that there were no dancers except Pearl Lang and me. Where were the boys and girls, now distinguished leaders of their profession, who had made Martha's career possible, who had fought beside her, worked for her, served her for four decades with loyalty, passion, nobility?

Where were they, the friends, the valiants, the ones that had made it all possible? Nelle Fisher, Anna Sokolow, Jane Dudley, Sophie Maslow, Pearl Lang? Well, she had come, the only one. But where were Merce Cunningham, Erick Hawkins (Martha's husband once), Paul Taylor, Mary Hinkson, Yuriko, Matt Turney, Bertram Ross?

They were all alive. They were all around. Where were they tonight at her honoring? What we had present was a paltry crew. This was the elite flotsam, the people who went to cocktail parties, got their names in the press, went to benefits, got on TV. How she had despised them! But where were the soldiers? Ah me! Martha was alone, standing beside the President of the United States, decorated and alone. My heart was filled with wonder and terror.

Martha looked ravishing in scarlet silk, like a Japanese empress, her black hair glossy and lacquered, tiny. (She came to Gerald Ford's shoulder and she came to Betty Ford's mouth. I had no idea that the president was so large and burly a presence. Martha was, beside him, a miniature deity.) And at the conclusion of the dinner, amid glassware and flowers, in front of the John Adams fireplace he hung the superb blue ribbon around her neck and on it the medallion of the Medal of Freedom, and he made an extremely good speech, probably the best he had made the whole of his Administration. Obviously it had been written by somebody who liked Martha and understood her, and I'm sure it was vetted by the First Lady. And then we adjourned to the East Ballroom. Martha spoke, as only she can, and then they put up on the little ballroom stage the Isamu Noguchi fence and the ropes designating the horizon, which was the set that changed theatrical history. One of her current soloists, flown in from Madrid, performed her *Lamentation* (1930) and her *Frontier* (1935). Well, it wasn't Martha, although all the steps and gestures were identical. But the sheer power of Martha Graham cannot be duplicated.

Byron and I walked to the hotel through the shuffling autumn leaves, our steps and my train rustling in the grass. And we had a nightcap. I had been very careful about my drinking and had confined myself to orange juice at the White House because I didn't wish to stumble any more than I had to.

Then it happened. Once again I was on the edge.

In the middle of the night I woke up extremely sick. I wanted to vomit. I couldn't vomit. I was hot. I had Pauline open all the windows. I couldn't get cool. I couldn't get my breath. I couldn't breathe, scarcely at all. I was sick and wanted to vomit and there was a weight on my right arm, pulling on it, pulling. This was all new and very uncomfortable.

"Pauline," I finally said, "you'd better get a doctor. Phone the desk." She was frightened. I could think of no one to wake up but Roger Stevens, and I scarcely thought I'd like to do that. There were many people in Washington who could have helped me, but I couldn't remember their names at the moment. The desk said they'd send around a doctor but it would take a little time, and I just sweated it out and Pauline became more and more frightened. He finally arrived, looking somewhat like a veterinarian. And I said, "Do you think I had better go to a hospital?"

And he said, "Do you want to?"

And I said, "No, of course I don't. I want to go home. But I have got to vomit."

"Well," he said, "I think I can make you vomit and I'm sure I can make you sleep. I think you're having a very bad gas attack."

Finally I said, "Do you think this could possibly be a heart attack?"

And he said, "Does it feel like it?"

And I stared at him blankly. "What does that feel like?"

And then he said, "It depends." With that helpful remark he gave me a pill and said, "If you don't feel better in the morning you'd better go to a hospital. If you feel well enough you'd better go home. And that will be twenty dollars. I'd like it in cash right now."

Dr. Plum explains:

Several kinds of difficulties beset hotel doctors. Except in the plushest places, many of them are there because the job is not too taxing. Others have been in poor health or otherwise have had difficulty meeting the demanding pace that the profession places on its practitioners. Also, many or most of the complaints that hotel doctors deal with represent no more than the transient outcries of a traveler whose physical or emotional pain will be gone by morning. In that kind of a setting the doctor would quickly lose his job if he overresponded to every minor ache. None of these considerations excuse this doctor's failure to recognize a potentially serious group of symptoms (or even inquire about Miss de Mille's past history of vascular disease). However, they may help the reader to understand why it can be difficult for a physician who spends 99 percent of his time dealing with superficial aches and pains abruptly to recognize in the middle of the night that a *particular* pain in a *particular* patient represents serious trouble and demands urgent attention.

I, too, feel sorry for poor old hacks but still do not think any of this is an excuse for failure to understand the difference between a heart attack and a drunken megrim.

The next morning the unsuspecting Byron came by for breakfast. I dispatched him to pay the hotel bill and to eat by himself. Pauline dressed me and I was taken downstairs. I felt worse. I sat in the lobby bowed over my cane. Byron took care of the bills and got a cab. We went to the airport. When we got there he found that our plane flight had been cancelled. We would have to go home by shuttle, which I wished to avoid because of the stairs and the long walk to a taxi. But I couldn't wait for another plane, sitting there hours at the airport. Last night's guests, fresh, chic, many in traveling togs and very smart, nodded at me. I did not look radiant. I looked like an old hag huddling in a bundle of clothes. And I was white to the lips. "Too much to drink," they thought. "She shouldn't go out to parties." I got home finally, miserable, and went to bed. By five o'clock that afternoon I had summoned the energy to phone Gorham.

"I'm sick," I said.

And he said, "Why don't you come up and see me immediately?"

"I wouldn't dream of it. I'm too sick to go out. I feel nauseated."

"No, I've had a better idea."

"What is that?"

"Get into the first cab you can find and rush to the

emergency ward." So that's what I did. They had me in a room and a strange doctor and Gorham came to me and as a matter of routine he first took a cardiogram.

"Wow!" he said.

"What?" said I, instantly terror-stricken.

"Well, you've got it. Here it is. Right here." And then he said, "Just stay quiet, absolutely quiet." And then in came a strange doctor in brown tweeds and he took another cardiogram and said, "What!! Yep. There it is."

And I said, "What?"

And he said, "You've had an incident. You're having a coronary."

"Impossible!" I protested indignantly. "I don't have heart trouble. Don't be silly. I have vascular trouble, as you well know."

"You've got heart trouble now," he said. "But don't worry." And then Gorham came back and held my hand and said, "You're going to be perfectly alright. Don't worry. But we've got to keep you here. No need to worry. And don't move."

"I can't go home?"

"No, I'm afraid not. You're going into intensive care this minute."

"Dammit!" I said. "That's what comes from having dinner with a Republican!" Nobody laughed.

I was being rolled away with all sorts of tubes attached to my wrists and a nurse at my head. And Walter was there. And Mary. Once more. Once again they were there, bending over me, kissing me, and Walter shaking and saying, "Oh, my darling, what have you done? What have you done to me?"

"I had dinner with a Republican." They didn't laugh either.

I was wheeled into a new intensive care room and this was a peculiar one because this was heterosexual, that is, there was a dying man in the next bed and a very sick boy across the aisle. Nobody cared a tuppence for proprieties. They went on trying to keep the little pumps working and that's all they cared about all night, and about asking questions, asking questions without end.

Dr. Plum comments:

> Although Agnes de Mille had never previously exhibited specific symptoms of serious heart disease, she did have hypertension. That disorder, if left untreated, places as much, or more, burden on the heart and its blood vessels as it does on the brain. Doctors know well, for example, that in patients with strokes the risk of future difficulties with the heart is at least as great as the risk of recurrent injury to the brain. When she first came to the emergency room, her electrocardiogram showed the characteristic changes of a limited injury to the wall of the heart. She had suffered what, in medical terms, is called a myocardial infarction or, less accurately, a coronary thrombosis. Although she felt decidedly unwell, neither her clinical condition nor the pattern of her heart's electrical abnormalities implied any immediate threat to her life. Nevertheless, even small heart attacks can interfere with the

heart's natural pumping action. More dangerously, the bruise in the heart can increase the muscle's irritability so as to interfere directly or indirectly with the delicate mechanisms that generate the organ's life-sustaining natural, regular rhythm. Emergency treatment can reverse these abnormalities, but in severe cases such treatment must come instantly if the patient's life is to be saved or the brain protected from damage.

After a heart attack the immediately heightened risks have led nearly all hospitals to institute in their midst special coronary care or critical care units. In such units painless instruments attached to the patient can sense each heartbeat and breath and continuously record these activities on large cathode-ray screens, along with other appropriate signs of bodily activity. Any change in these vital functions immediately reflects itself in an abnormal squiggle on the screen. To make sure of attracting attention, an alarm bell alerts the constantly available, highly trained staff. Such measures detect life-threatening episodes within fractions of seconds of their onset, so that the medical-nursing team can restore the patient's circulation to the voraciously demanding brain and other life-sustaining organs. By means of such procedures thousands of lives are saved.

Not surprisingly, given the density of equipment and the highly trained people required to meet the human emergencies and operate the machines, hospital intensive care units are hideously expensive to operate. So expensive, in fact, that no hospital nowadays can afford to keep men and women patients apart in an intensive care unit if it means leaving a bed empty that could serve someone who needs the supervision. So, such high technology areas usually are indiscriminately unisex in their clientele.

I can assure the medical staff that that night I could not have cared if the adjacent patient had three legs or eighteen sex organs. I felt rotten.

"Do you feel? Can you remember? What happened then?"

"Dammit," I said. "Let me sleep."

"Just answer. Just answer these questions."

In the morning I was given something perfectly nondescript to eat, without a bit of salt.

"What is it?" I said.

"It doesn't matter. It's enough nourishment. Get it down if you can."

"What is the matter with me?"

"Don't talk. Just answer the question first and then be quiet."

A day later they had me in a room with four women, so I had been promoted to a women's ward of a kind. The food remained revolting. And all new doctors, an entirely new breed, new faces, the very best experts in their field. Looking down at my untouched lunch, one said, "I think that's stupid food to give you."

"So do I," I said.

"You have to cut it and you have to chew it and you haven't the strength."

"And I haven't the will."

"Understandable." But it wasn't changed and there was no salt.

The difference between a little salt and no salt is crucial. It is the difference between pleasantly edible and cardboard.

I finally managed the strength to call Byron Belt and apologize. "I wasn't malingering on that plane with you. It was a coronary attack and I'm in the hospital. And please don't mention this in your newspaper." And that gallant gentleman never did. To this moment it has never been spoken of. And he was a newspaperman!

On the fourth day they moved me out of the coronary care unit to a room with one roommate, an enchanting woman who had drastic surgery and was very sick indeed (she was having a colostomy), but was able to talk, and talk pleasantly and talk quietly.

I had given orders that nobody should know that I was sick again. I didn't even tell Margaret, not wanting to frighten her. I told mighty few. It seemed I was getting to be a real bore, a redundancy. Again? Again, yet again? Yessiree, over and over. The doctors weren't really frightened as far as I knew, but they were firm. I had a minimum of flowers and very few phone calls and I thrashed to get out, to get back to my rehearsals.

The Robert Joffrey company was doing my ballet *Rodeo* for the first time and Vernon Lusby was in charge of all rehearsals. I should have been there with him. I wasn't. He came up to see me and at the most peculiar times. And I said, "You mustn't come at these hours. These are not visiting hours."

And he said, "I come when I'm not on the rehearsal floor and you know it. I have no choice." And he had none. I gave him all the instructions I could and we kept in touch on the telephone. But I wasn't there. They needed me desperately. Well, they couldn't have me. Vernon continued to confer at the hospital. We got close to opening night. I begged to go.

"Certainly not."

And so Walter took Kate and they had the gala without me. Vernon took a bow. I'm very glad for this because he'd carried the brunt of the work alone. All the dancers and Joffrey and Vernon grabbed the backstage telephone as soon as the curtain fell and telephoned me. The lady in the next bed sat up. It was quite late for her and, indeed, quite late for me.

"How did it go? How did it go?" she asked just as if she had been in the profession a long time.

"A triumph, no less! A real honest-to-God triumph."

And it had been, it seems, a beautiful, a really beautiful, dazzling performance. And then finally Vernon and the dancers hung up and the phone rang again instantly and it was Walter across the street at a restaurant with Kate.

"Who have you been talking to? It was marvelous, marvelous!" But it was without me. All this was going on without me. I was not part of it. I was posthumous.

So I was now respected, revered even, treated tenderly

as I never had been before, but I was actually a relic, a
fetish held up as a token at tribal rites, while the partici-
pants, the hot-blooded young men, who had no time or
energy to pay heed, took over. Professionally I would be
neglected and disregarded. There was not much time left.
Oh peace and quiet of heart!

I had my manuscript brought up. It was now at a point
where I was talking to Kate's secretary and spreading out
the papers all over the floor. And one day my roommate
said to me, "Miss de Mille, I think you will have to realize
that this is a hospital and not the editorial office of a
newspaper." The nurse had been unable to get in with a
tray. So I had to move to the solarium, which was, of
course, not convenient, with people there marching all
over, all over the papers and all over the notes, but we
paid no attention to them, nor did they to us, except to
complain about having to walk on all those papers.

One day there were spots in front of my eyes. Well,
what of that? Nothing. Everybody sees spots from time to
time. I always do when I have a stomach upset. But du-
tifully I reported to Dr. Gorham. The balance of the
blood was all wrong, it seemed. The recipe was incorrect.
They wouldn't be responsible for anything that happened.

"What could happen?"

"IT, all over." Gorham, the darling, was adamant. "A
heart muscle is involved. You have strained a muscle. You
have to let it heal. Crucial. You cannot move from your

bed or make any effort. And we must try to get your
blood straightened out."

"But I feel fine."

"That's good, but you see spots."

Dr. Plum was away at this time, I think in San Fran-
cisco, or it may have been in Washington or Atlanta or
even abroad. He went all over the place getting money
for his school and learning things. For instance, once during my direst time he went to Washington for two days.

"You be good," he said. "Don't do anything I wouldn't
want you to. I have to get a million dollars."

And when he returned I said, "Did you get it?"

And he said, "Oh, sure."

Another time, along with the experts from Harvard and
Columbia, he went to Iran (but this was before I knew
him) and advised the Shah on how to build a hospital system; between them—the Shah and his advisors—they had
cured the country of tuberculosis of the spine, that
scourge that had littered the floors of the bazaars with
crablike, crawling creatures who scrabbled in the dirt for
pennies and lived as outcasts from hell. Absolutely cured,
finished. This is something the Ayatollah fails to mention.
Well, Plum came back this time, lured perhaps by the
spots, and very glad I was to see him.

This is what he said:

Actually—and hardly surprising, given all she had been
through—this episode of the heart attack stands out in
Miss de Mille's memory more fearsomely than it appeared

medically at the time. From the time she arrived at The
New York Hospital she improved steadily, without hesitation or relapse. Much of her strength and vivacity resur-
faced within a matter of a few days, and neither by symptom nor laboratory test did her heart show further injury.
She left the hovering attention of intensive care by the
fourth day and thereafter physically exercised with in-
creasing vigor, at first in bed, then sitting, and finally
walking by the eleventh day after the onset of her pain.
When she was acutely ill, Dr. Gorham had wisely given
her the anticoagulant heparin to prevent any acute recurrence of blood clotting in the legs. On day thirteen the
drug acted too strongly and she had a small nosebleed
and a bloodshot eye, but by then the major danger had
passed and the heparin was first reduced and ultimately
stopped on the seventeenth day, when she went home,
ready to resume her place in the dance.

At the conclusion of this episode I went home, none the
worse, it seems, but with an added pill to take four times
a day and nitroglycerin to carry in my purse just in case.
Walter said to me, "I have written a letter I want you
to read. I'm very pleased with it." I append the letter.

October 25, 1976

Dear Dr. ——

This is to acknowledge with thanks your services
to my wife, Agnes de Mille Prude, on October

15th, at the ———— when you treated her for nausea and advised her to return to New York.

It may be instructive for you to know that what
you were witnessing that morning was a classic
coronary attack that might easily have proven
fatal under your treatment. The foregoing is not
my opinion but that of doctors at the emergency
cardiac unit of [The] New York Hospital, where
my wife was admitted on advice of her New
York physician on Friday afternoon upon her
arrival here from Washington.

Trusting this information may be useful to you
and your patients on future occasions,

                              Yours sincerely,

                              Walter Prude

WP/rs

There was no reply.

Moral: Do not call in hotel doctors. If you are
sufficiently alive, go to the hospital. You may have to stay
there, but the risk of travelling in taxis and airplanes and
walking—walking downstairs, walking upstairs in the
middle of a full coronary attack—is grave, and when I
tell this story medical men turn white and their wives
close their eyes and say, "Oh God!"

I discovered, on going home, that I could walk down

rakes and slopes and that I could walk without a cane. I could even walk downstairs with a minimum loss of balance. No doctor has attempted to explain this.

Another startling phenomenon that grew out of my experiences was that I no longer had headaches. Formerly I had them nightly, daily, sometimes with the intensity of migraine. I ate Empirin like mints. Now no more, not one. So here we find a prime cure for headaches: cerebral hemorrhage. It is, however, not recommended.

So that was that. I was going to stay alive for a bit.

To what good? Not just to make daily fertilizer.

I was a destroyed body but I felt young because I felt fresh, with a new way of looking at things. I hadn't tried for this metamorphosis. It happened. Who could tell what my ideas or my feelings would be? Not I. Like lost seeds in the dark, in well-used old ground there were now things growing, just as in the London blitz fireweed grew on the charred ruins, field flowers sprouted on the floor of the Stock Exchange, the Wool Market, the Bank of England; sixteenth- and seventeenth-century flowers long buried under the black cellars of the city blasted up from the subrefuse, subsoot depths, long lost, Shakespeare's flowers, before that, Spencer's, dormant these many hundred years and now freed and colorful in the air, with the colors and style Henry the Fifth had seen. Just so, the pavements of my life had been broken, the habits smashed, the hurry, the clamor, all the constraints that had pushed me down (try, try harder, try again and harder, keep trying harder, better). And I was burnt and twisted but freed, and this without trying, without wishing, without even knowing, so that unexpectedly there were ideas, perceptions to explore and with no fear, for, indeed, nothing more now could happen to me except extinction. Nothing more could be lost except love, and that would not be (and don't forget that, ever). And God granted that I was aware of all of this. That is the very secret. That is the whole meaning. I knew.

What lay ahead? Open the window.

Thoreau said it better: "The light which puts out our eyes is darkness to us. Only that day dawns to which we are awake. There is more day to dawn. The sun is but a morning star."

Meanwhile Mag, the indomitable girl, not only stole time out between her hideous medical exercises to go to Cuernavaca in the early summer, but she now proposed to go to Italy with her daughter to visit her granddaughter. But, in truth, she was exhausted and she began to know it. Frequently she was in pain, and there were times on the Via Veneto when she had to stop and sit down at a little coffee table simply to gather the strength to go to the end of the block. But she persisted. In the Blue Grotto of Capri she lost her wig. It caught on a jagged rock in the very low ceiling and the boat sailed on, leaving it behind. But then it kindly stopped on the way back to retrieve it. Margaret found all this hilarious and told it with great gusto when she returned. With great gusto? Well, not quite. With amusement, sly and muted. Great gusto she had no longer, her sudden booming laugh no more. She was still the smartest lady in Maryland, and wherever she went she dazzled people. And she was always fun. "I'm the belle of Belsen!" she said as she adjusted scarves and neckerchiefs and blouses to hide the bones which suddenly showed in her chest and shoulders and the scrawny strings of her beautiful throat. When the hair situation got drastic she wore a little eighteenth-century lace cap in the hospital where she couldn't wear a wig, and she looked like a Boucher drawing, absolutely irresistible.

But she was doomed.

I knew she was dying. It was like a pedal point to everything that played in my life—morning and night—the strange, gaping certainty, the little sister, the younger one in the process of being destroyed.

Margaret was going, but out of her loss and mine I had found her again, and she me. I thought of her in my quiet as I lay resting, waiting. Did she me as she lay gazing at the bare branches of her garden in Maryland, so far away, gazing around her lovely bedroom with its fine artifacts and silver-framed photographs and the portrait of her painted by President Eisenhower? And as I lay, staring at the October apartment fronts opposite, did the same memories come back to both? Probably, because we were sisters again.

And because we had time once more, as when we were young. This is what had been given to us out of our loss:

the ability to see what was there, savor it, notice it, notice everything. We had to wait so often now! But there was the light, the colors changing, the sounds. In fact, we were given back the world, the whole intricate, lovely world after the hubbub of the busyness. It was like the eighteenth century, a new scale of light and sound. Back then they took time. It was there and they took it. And that is why they wrote so well and they knew so well how to build houses and countries. And they knew one another.

The world was peopled, as it was now suddenly for me.

PART THREE

Challenge

---

*I couldn't be the person I am now
without the imprisonment.*

—BARRY ROSEN,
*former hostage in
Iran (1979–1981)*

XIX

MY EIGHTEENTH-CENTURY serenity was only now and then, and in between, from instinct and habit, I fretted to be active. Up, up, out of the torpor. To horse and away.

I did not yearn to rejoin the Broadway parade, nor to force my name back in the market, but to rejoin the living, the doers.

Let me try to be clear, because I think this is important. All those capabilities and activities which I was so used to—the freedom to drive myself wherever I wanted to; to go alone where I wished to (the theater, movies, lectures, rehearsals, trips, dinners, shopping, whatever); the ability to do alone whatever had to be done; the policing up of my own house (mending, cleaning, washing, cooking, whatever I wanted to do); as well as those more animal exercises (running, walking, jumping, ah! and, oh yes, dancing), gone, gone. Denied me suddenly and absolutely. I never regretted them except in moments of frustration and irritation. I could accept the loss of these. I never yearned to have them back because I couldn't, simply, and therefore there was no choice. But in those concerns where there was a possibility of achievement, where there was a possibility of choice and an undetermined path, there I yearned to be active, to be alive, to be, as the Buddha said, AWAKE. And I felt that I must not, could not, willed not to just shut my eyes and sleep, accepting in these matters also total cessation.

Robert Joffrey's reconstruction of *Rodeo* having proved thunderingly successful, I approached him with the idea that we do my *Conversations About the Dance*, which had been so abruptly interrupted by the stroke. I proposed that this time we do it with full orchestra and his company and all the resources of his school. It would be a big undertaking. It would also be risky. He agreed.

The risks were on several levels. There would be a cast of well over forty people and new costumes to see to. We had used only a solo pianist, David Baker, for all previous performances. This time I augmented the music by adding forty-five instruments, and all the music, all that was suitable, was orchestrated by Elizabeth Meyer specially for the occasion. We added excerpts from *Rodeo* and the first section of Jerome Robbins' *Interplay*, from the Joffrey repertory, with full costumes and company. We added many fine dancers, brilliant soloists: Denise Jackson, Russell Saltzbach, Paul Sutherland, Janet Eilber. For the corps de ballet numbers, the old historical pieces, I employed the Joffrey II group, their second group of apprentices, who were young in age—between sixteen and eighteen—and adorably charming and able. Only a few of my stalwarts were left over from the old company—Gemze de Lappe, Honi Coles, Mel Tomlinson, James Jamieson, the fiddler-caller James Morrison, Ilene Strickler, Judith Epstein, David Evans and Cynthia Penn—but on the whole it was new dancers.

The first thing I had to do was to renovate my costumes, all of which, together with the scenery, were stored in a school, where, I discovered, they had been, in large part, stolen or destroyed. The school official in charge explained:

"When we heard how sick you were, we took it for granted that you would not be wanting your costumes again [this is a euphemism for you know what] and, being pressed for space, we made room for our own properties. We wrote you about this matter, but as you never replied we assumed you were in agreement." There was no letter. In effect, what they had done was burn the scenery (seen on bonfires by witnesses), annex most of the costumes ripped from baskets and boxes, and allow the students to rampage through the properties and simply take, that is, steal whatever they fancied!

This was not only a break of trust, a financial loss of forty-two thousand dollars, but a horrid introduction to the unattractive experience of being defunct, and I raged. My lawyer proving to be both careless and negligent, the insurance company paid only a token fee. It was criminal

and it was shocking, but it was a two-year-old fact. I had
work ahead. Let it go.

"Do not fret about anything," said the doctors.

And, in fact, nothing mattered except working, staying
alive and working.

The lecture material now had to be adapted to a seden-
tary figure who could not move at all. I tried my little
jokes in front of a mirror and I couldn't do them, not even
with somebody holding my hand and supporting my
waist, not when they involved the torso. The fun was
gone.

The rehearsals went well. The young dancers were
beautiful children, enthusiastic and respectful. They tried
with all their might to learn style. Ballet dancers today
are taught one style only—late, Romantic, nineteenth-
century Russian balletic ballet—no other, no character or
folk dancing of any kind. They are not so versatile or so
roundly trained as the generations preceding. But these
children did listen and they did try and they did learn.
Their courtesy and enthusiasm were like medicine to me.
I found myself beginning to move freely, to use my hand
as I had not done recently, and to use my arm.

Judy Epstein got out my notes from May 15, 1975, and
I my prestroke videotapes made in the Harkness House.
But there was need for new choreography, and this presented us all with an entirely new problem. The teaching
of any dance role is done by rote since we do not commonly use a script. There are scripts—the Labannotation
here and the Benesh choreology in England—but because

both are very difficult to learn and practice dancers and choreographers are not usually versed in them. The steps therefore must be shown and imitated and dancers have grown remarkably adept in the skills of noticing, analyzing and duplicating, as well as remembering. (Their memories are prodigious. I would say dancers are far sharper than any police and would make expert witnesses at a murder trial.)

But they must first be shown what is wanted, and there I was, so to speak, mute and forced to demonstrate verbally. Now there is nothing whatever that cannot be described in the English language, but we are not used to thinking exactly, not in the dance world. "Lift the foot before," one demands. But is one speaking in time or space? Do you mean in the air or on the ground, or at what degree of the arc? In terms of height or laterally? With what flexion of the knee? With what dynamics? Sharply, softly, slowly or fast? With what relation to the legs of the next person? To the arms? Indeed, you have to speak as precisely as a mathematician. I learned how. It was difficult, but I learned. The dancers were very patient and we all learned together.

And then there was the matter of a whole new group of black girls whom I had added to the show. Joffrey did not have such a contingent within his corps de ballet, so I borrowed them from New York's School of Performing Arts, and very young, half-trained, charming children came up to me to be taught. Glory Van Scott, who had been one of my soloists in the Heritage Theater, took

them on as her charge. One day she was going on like
thunder, doing some wonderful kick-prances in the old
cakewalk style, when she suddenly fell flat on the ground.
I said jocosely, "Well, if your instructor can manage to do
that split kick again without tripping herself up, we'll
continue." And then I noticed that Glory was writhing in
spasms. I started up but I couldn't get to her, although I
tried to. The others did. They summoned help. Boys came
in and carried her off the floor. Glory had thrown her
knee right out of joint, so vigorous and enthusiastic had
been her cake-kick, and she didn't walk again without
crutches for nine months. It was a terrifying half hour. So
Glory was taken away and we had to get someone else
who kicked more discreetly. The girls learned their piece
and were very, very moving indeed. Such episodes are not
unusual in rehearsal stints. They happen frequently and
one must prepare for them. But they are always shocking
to behold, to experience and to cope with.

So we proceeded, week by week, and the staff worked
doggedly at advertising and selling.

I was happy to be in the thick again, but, of course, I
was also scared. There is always trepidation before a public performance. In this case the hazards were special. I
had been off the stage for nearly two years and there was
considerable curiosity about how the catastrophe had left
me! Had I grown old? White-haired, yes, but decrepit?
Was I, in fact, alive?

The City Center Opera House has a capacity of 2,932
seats, very much larger than anything I had ever spoken

in before. The Hunter College Playhouse had held less than seven hundred seats and we had filled that with effort. But three thousand! Quite a different problem. My small foundation had some money saved. We raised some more. Joffrey and I pooled our resources.

Everyone of note in New York would be attending, and this time it really would be everyone, including all the press. Expecting what? Also, there would be all the big foundations that I had vainly summoned before, and they were vital to continuance.

Before the stroke I had given one concert and lost six thousand dollars, but I was enthusiastically persuaded to repeat it by the heads of IBM, who had heard of it and promised to attend this one. They sent their secretaries. The secretaries reported we had a smash hit. The bosses said, "Please do another." But the price had gone up. It was now ten thousand. I didn't have an extra ten thousand and the company had been dispersed. We had had to wait. We had had to wait until May 15, and on May 15 they had all the important viewers assembled in the Hunter College Playhouse.

Now, two and a half years later for this November night in the New York City Center Auditorium, the foundations had agreed to come back; the public television station Channel 13 in New York also said they'd come; and all the heads of the Shubert Foundation, the Rockefeller Foundation and the Ford Foundation. If all went well, the idea was to televise the performance and get it on PBS. This time, in very truth, they were there, but with an attention not only to artistic and professional values but—something new in my experience—clinical considerations, because they were not only looking for talent but durability, for much as they applauded my courage they guarded their investments and they were not going to be enticed into sentimental risk just because I showed a streak of stubborn gallantry.

I had heard on fairly good authority that someone at WNET with high responsibility had stated that I was certainly not up to the concert, nor to making a TV show of the concert, and that anyone who hazarded a penny on such an enterprise was a fool. And doors were closed, very quietly and rather secretly and politely, but firmly and finally.

There were other disturbing considerations. My speech had slurred and thickened. My mind was slower than it had been, my tongue far less nimble. And then there was the question of my stamina. I was now subject to sudden fatigues, fatigues that I had never known before. They came on me as hunger assails a child, after only two hours of effort. It was as if somebody had turned a light off. I didn't begin to get tired. I was suddenly exhausted, had to stop whatever I was doing and lie down. How could I maintain the disciplines with these handicaps?

But the real hazard I did not mention to anyone or even name to myself: I was frightened for my very safety. On the last occasion involving such a speech I had had a massive cerebral hemorrhage, and since that time I had had very bad mental lapses, two or three of them, and the heart prank. With this occasion duplicating in all ways the strains of May 15, 1975, but adding some extra strain under the heading of our grandiose augmentation, would these added challenges produce a tension that would do me down? Would I have a second stroke, possibly a coronary attack? Would I have a mental lapse, so that in the middle of a sentence I would find myself unable to finish and simply babble? The evening was two hours long. I was to be on the stage for the duration. Was I up to it? Could I ask myself to be? And there was to be no complete full dress run-through, no preview, no pretrial, no warm-up. Why not? We couldn't afford it. And I didn't have the energy.

Walter was frightened and said so. He put his entire will against the idea.

"Why must you?" he said. "Why must you risk further? Why disturb the placidity we now know? It's a form of vanity." And, indeed, I suppose it may have been. But as I had to live, I felt I had to function the best way I knew how.

I proceeded by dumb animal instinct, as plants turn to light, as animals to oxygen. I needed activity. I must DO.

Walter suffered.

Passivity is not a man's natural role. This is what I had had to endure during the war. But then, of course, it was *force majeure* and must be submitted to willy-nilly. No choice. Now he was being asked to stand back and let me walk deliberately into danger, to risk incompetence, speechlessness, yes, even death—to gain what? I knew, I

knew. And it was not just another Broadway success but
the sense of living and the rejoining of the active human
race.

I had two solo sessions each with Gorham and Plum.
Gorham said, "You seem alright to me as far as I can
tell. I cannot predict exactly, of course. You're not twenty.
You're not even fifty, and you've been through dreadful
experiences. But as far as any instruments show, you will
be able to do this if you feel you will be."

"I do," I said.

And Plum said, "You cannot live your life as though
you were going to die. You will die, of course, and possibly sooner now than before. But you must live as though
you will live. This is not a bad risk."

In my stress I phoned Margaret. "If the doctors say
Okay, go ahead. What else can you do? I would if I could
in your place."

"If I could I would."

Lost, lovely woman! She flashed handsomely by, laughing, making us laugh, dazzling of skin, blue of eye, with
the piercing gaze of a child beneath a high, tortured
brow; flirting her graces and pretendings and in the very
second of the pretty flummery naming herself with honesty, lean and terse. Brave Mag! You never flinched. The
grace and stylishness of your courage we shall not look on
soon again.

Her death was to be later in the spring, but now she
said, "Take your courage in your hands and do it."

Not all my friends and associates were of a single mind.

They said nothing, but their worry was very real. Walter's apprehension—no, his terror—remained extreme. Yet he bowed to my need.

"I'll help," he said.

Suddenly I was aware of what I was asking of him, of the courage demanded of his discipline. We never spoke again on this matter, but he knew I knew.

Physically I got stronger. The effort made me stronger and the habit of doing things right. I went to company dance rehearsals every day, promptly, and raised hell for two or three hours and went home and had my tea and slept. And that was a day's work done.

I bought tickets for my doctors, Gorham and Plum and McCagg, and I knew where they were to be seated so that if anything happened they could be summoned backstage instantly. And I asked James Mitchell in Los Angeles to cross the continent to stand beside me in the wings with the extra script so that in case I collapsed he could slip into my chair and simply read and the show would go on this time and would not come to a sickening halt. The audience could be told afterward that I was out of sorts.

But whatever happened, this was to be my golden night! My resurrection. Unique among the thousands I had lived.

I knew this performance would be without match whatever happened, so I asked to have it videotaped for the New York Public Library's archive. The dancers' union, AGMA, balked; not even history was to be re-

corded without pay. If they got paid the musicians and
stagehands wanted full recompense. So this project was
abandoned. Accordingly, I asked for an audiotape only
and the musicians' union agreed. *Mirabile dictu!* Just before curtain a little man arrived with full equipment and
authority he claimed from the dance archives of the Lincoln Center branch of the New York Public Library. Gerald Arpino, codirector with Robert Joffrey, gave up his
own seats—the best in the house, front-row balcony center
—to accommodate him. At the conclusion of this exercise
the little man was to thank everyone courteously and
disappear. Forever. And the tape has never surfaced, although we searched illegal and bootleg outlets. All proving that Paradise has leaky ceilings.

The company blessedly knew nothing of my worries.
They had seen me in rehearsal and they knew that I was
physically unsteady, but they knew nothing more. Also,
they had no idea what the performance would be like, not
having heard me speak except in rehearsal, informally,
muttering and calling. They had never heard me say a
finished sentence, so they were rather bewildered by the
entire proceedings and probably pleasantly curious in an
apathetic way, interested only in doing their dance steps
correctly.

Mrs. Mondale, the Vice-President's wife, said that she
would come to this hazardous, extraordinary, problem-
atical evening. (She was the key to the National Endow-
ment for the Arts and she meant to help.) Well, it was do
or die. The proper seats were procured for her and her

party and for her FBI bodyguards, who had to sit directly behind her. And the proper publicity was sent out.

On the big night Walter was white around the lips, but he said nothing and he went off to get ready and I went to the theater.

Pauline and I went to the dressing room, Joffrey's own, and there were flowers there for me, but I ordered them to be brought in afterward. In a certain way this was to be like an operating room.

I went down to the stage very early and sat there; the beloved environment, the beloved country, the dancers in makeup with woolen leggings tied over their tights to keep them warm, warming up and trying steps and trying holds and positions; the stagehands extraordinarily courteous to me for the first time in my whole life, solicitous. "Watch where you step. Look out for this cable. There's a light stand there. Let me have your hand." And flashing torches on wires and braces, Joffrey hovering around like a beneficent bumblebee, small, with a can of hair spray in his hands, pushing loose strands of the girls' hair back into place, patting girls' hair, fixing their dresses, watching. He is not a fusser. This was a nervous release for him and for them, and he was there with them watching every gesture. "Throw your legs higher on that lift. Try to get the balance lower in the hips. Lean forward and you'll spin longer. Have some spray."

Suddenly we were all told that Mrs. Mondale's limousine had turned in from Seventh Avenue and was coming down Fifty-sixth Street, and that she would stop backstage on her way out to the auditorium. We were all lined up and hordes, literally scores of press people came with their official tickets tied on and stood beside police and cameramen. And there were batteries of public media personnel and all I could think of was, dear God, let me keep my wits about me, let me be quiet in my heart.

And then we were told that Mrs. Mondale was indeed turning down Fifty-sixth Street, and then that Mrs. Mondale was at the door of the theater, the back door. And, in fact, she did come up the back steps, the same ones that I had gone up so often with the help of the dear, lame, black guard who made it his business to see that I got properly put in the elevator and looked after by the other guards, and who gave me advice about how to walk and how to protect myself. She came past him and she came past my elevators, and there she was, the good, gentle lady with her immediate entourage. And she came to me and I rose up on the arms of my dancers and made my courtesies. And she said charming things and I answered charmingly. Keep your mind on what you're going to say. Don't be diverted. Don't be disturbed. "Thank you, Mrs. Mondale. You're too kind." What will the opening sentences be? How do you follow up? Supposing they don't laugh. "I hope your seats are alright." Supposing they don't applaud when you enter? Oh, how chilling! You must be sure of yourself, so that you go ahead no matter what happens. Mrs. Mondale was taken into the auditorium and we got about our business.

There were a few minutes more left to become quiet

again and acclimated to a professional backstage atmosphere and to forget the press and all the outlanders streaming around. But she was there alright and the evening was official.

We had to get on with it. We did get on with it.

Lights were changing. Lights were being tested with new colored gelatins. "Is this microphone the right height for you?" Jim Mitchell arrived. I gave him one script and asked him to stand at stage right. Walter had given him a thermos of tea just in case my throat closed up. He also had a phial of nitroglycerin in his pocket. Mary Green had another script and was at stage left. But since we had been through the very complicated program only once, she thought she'd better stand there and check the dancers on and off in the proper sequence. She literally called the show like a square dance.

Beyond the curtain was the astonishing rustle of the crowd, which an experienced ear can detect as either a full audience, half an audience or an empty house; and either happy or nervous. This one was full and this one was excited. It murmured and rose. It is an extraordinary sound, muffled by the curtain, unlike any other. Bob Joffrey took my hand and we stood. The stage manager signalled us and the barrier swished up and there was a rush of air. And there was absolute silence and electric emptiness and waiting.

Applause, I guess. And then Bob seated me and I began to speak.

Would I remember? Would I hold onto myself? I said

the first two sentences without notes and there was a
cracking laugh, as sharp as a blow on my back, as sharp
as a hand extended over an abyss. I took the hand. I continued. Another. They were with me. They were ahead of
me. They intended that I succeed. They would not let me
fail. With that collaboration from the audience I knew I
could not show weakness or uncertainty. They expected
me to be excellent, and so I obliged them. We did it together. Every hesitation they waited out with humor and
courtesy and understanding. They exploded at the amusing points. I had to wait for them to recover. Never ever
in my entire life had I experienced such support and car-
ing from a body of people. And when the dancers came
out and performed the lovely old Jacobean numbers, they
had faces like roses and the boys were gallant and the audience was pleased. And so was I. And so were the performers. And then they got into the meat of the evening
and the soloists appeared; James Jamieson and Honi
Coles, Gemze de Lappe, and they delivered the way great
soloists do.

The company began to hear me talk. They heard the
remarks and they heard the astonishing response and they
were surprised and delighted and extremely stimulated.
They laughed spontaneously.

And we were through the first half and it was intermission.

I changed from the old red dress which I had worn as a
talisman. (I wore exactly the same costume I was to have
worn on May 15, 1975, jewel for jewel, the beautiful,

dark, blood-red dress that Stanley Simmons had designed
for me. The shoes were different because I could not wear
heels and I had to have a brace on my right leg. That was
different.) I put on the new beautiful dress Stanley had
made for me, reds of all tones, like the heart of a rose, like
flame, my Phoenix dress, and we started the second half
and it was simply grand. And at the end, when I shouted

"Honor your partner.
Honor your corner"

I threw out both hands to the audience, *both*, the right as
well as the left, extended and held open, a perfectly natural and spontaneous gesture. Caroline McCagg, sitting
just below me, drew in her breath so sharply that her
neighbors thought she was in pain and looked around
concerned. And she burst into tears. I had never used the
right arm before.

"'Cos now I'm through
And so are you!"

And the curtain came down.

I couldn't hear and I couldn't see, but the whole cast
stood there as planned, as rehearsed, and took their bows
and then Joffrey led me out to the center and I'm told the
entire audience rose on one count, spontaneously. But I
couldn't see or hear because of the lights.

I had gone white since my illness. I could not walk forward and I could not bow. But I could stand and I could
acknowledge. And the flowers came. Flowers and flowers.

And because I couldn't hold or carry anything, they were laid at my feet. Jim Mitchell came out with a great bunch of roses and laid them at my feet. At this point my agent, Biff Liff of the William Morris Agency, burst into tears because Jim was a star and he came without announcement or fanfare or place in the line of soloists. Bob Joffrey fixed a tiny, old-fashioned nosegay in my right hand. It was very light and very small, so that he thought that I could hold it and then he suddenly said, "Leave her."

And they scrambled. A voice hissed from the wings, "Be ready to catch her if she falls." David Baker, the pianist, was heard. "She's not going to fall."

I had no cane. I had no arm. I had no support. I had no companions. I was alone out there, absolutely alone. And the curtain went up and I stood exposed. And all I could think of was, "Let me not drop the bouquet." I stood alone and Walter's eyes filled with excitement. Fred Plum bit his lips. I stood without wobbling. I extended my arms again and the right arm did not waver. I held it high. And I did not drop the bouquet.